Alex Pettes
Nov 2011

Additional Praise for **Brand New**

"Maddock Douglas was first to market with the Agency of Innovation model making this book a must-read for any executive seeking the theory and tactics that today's 'next level' companies are utilizing to incorporate innovation strategies into their everyday practices."

—Marc Roth, President, Home Warranty of America, Inc.

"As a serial entrepreneur, I look at innovation as a silver bullet. Whether you sell software, energy or insurance, the ability to efficiently hit your mark with relevant ideas is the difference between profits and losses. Want more silver bullets? Read this book."

—Tim Stojka, CEO, Agentis Energy

"Don't go near this book, let alone open it, if you are looking for the same old answers. Mike and his team rarely visit 'inside the box' and, as a result, their ideas and clients tend to more quickly and profitably enter new markets and usher in new products better than the competition. Short of hiring the Maddock team, read the book and keep it away from your competitors. Then, get ready to go to the bank!"

—Jack Daly, CEO, Professional Sales Coach, Inc.

"I have worked with Mike and his team in a variety of diverse categories, applying their creative approach to innovation. Now this book lays it out for all to benefit and drive innovation through their organizations. A wonderful compass for all leaders."

—Christine Robins, CEO, BodyMedia

"This book will teach you how to reinvent the value proposition of even the most conservative industries using a proven, outside-in approach that is truly something wonderful."

—Greg Cohen, President, Moneris Solutions

Brand New

Brand New

SOLVING THE INNOVATION PARADOX—HOW GREAT BRANDS INVENT AND LAUNCH NEW PRODUCTS, SERVICES, AND BUSINESS MODELS

G. Michael Maddock and Luisa C. Uriarte
with Javier Flaim and Brett S. Miller of
Maddock Douglas—The Agency of Innovation

With a special thanks to Paul B. Brown

WILEY

John Wiley & Sons, Inc.

Published by John Wiley & Sons, Inc., Hoboken, New Jersey.
Published simultaneously in Canada.

Wiley also publishes its books in a variety of electronic formats. Some content that
appears in print may not be available in electronic books. For more information
about Wiley products, visit our web site at www.wiley.com.

Library of Congress Cataloging-in-Publication Data:

Maddock, G. Michael, 1965-
    Brand new : solving the innovation paradox—how great brands invent
and launch new products, services, and business models / G. Michael
Maddock, et al.
        p.   cm.
    Includes index.
    ISBN 978-0-470-64359-4 (cloth); ISBN 978-1-118-09593-5 (ebk);
    ISBN 978-1-118-09594-2 (ebk); ISBN 978-1-118-09595-9 (ebk)
        1. Technological innovations.   2. New products.   3. Creative ability in
business.   I. Uriarte, Luisa C., 1968- II. Flaim, Javier, 1970-
III. Miller, Brett S., 1969- IV. Brown, Paul B., 1954- V. Title.
HD45.M225   2011
658.5'75—dc22
                                                                    2011005631
Printed in the United States of America

10 9 8 7 6 5 4 3 2 1

Contents

Foreword

As the founder of the Entrepreneurs' Organization and also Gazelles, a fast-growth business consultancy, my life's work has been devoted to helping aggressive entrepreneurial companies scale. This has given me the opportunity to work with legendary entrepreneurs from the moment they had their big idea to the time they booked their first $100 million in revenue (and moved far beyond).

Typically, people start businesses in fields they know. They are working for a firm; spot an opportunity their company can't/won't take advantage of and go off to do it themselves.

But today, there is a different phenomena that is much more fascinating. A significant number of companies—everything from Amazon to Zip cars—are being started by "beginners"; people with no relevant industry background. (Jeff Bezos, creator of Amazon was a "rocket scientist" on Wall Street. Zip Car founder Robin Chase's background was in international health.)

Why is this significant? Bezos, Chase, and thousands like them are bringing multiple advantages to the table. First, they are not hamstrung by industry best-practices. (They don't know what they are.) They don't follow "the rules" about distribution/sales channels. (Again, because they simply are unaware of them.) And they don't know that what they are trying to do can't be done, because they never asked an "expert."

From my experience, established firms tend to dismiss the success of these types as having beginner's luck. But it is clearly more than that: It is a new way of looking at existing problems.

This is where Mike Maddock starts. I met Mike over a decade ago and have enjoyed being part of his innovation journey. His work has lead to the creation of a brand new category—the innovation agency—which is at its roots a proven process to help big companies act like entrepreneurs; he helps them act like beginners. It is this thinking that Mike and his team deliver in *Brand New*.

Want to make your company behave like the entrepreneurs that should be keeping you up at night? Read this book.

VERNE HARNISH
CEO, Gazelles

About the Authors

G. Michael Maddock is the founding partner and CEO of the leading innovation agency Maddock Douglas, which has helped 25 percent of the Fortune 100® invent, brand, and launch new products, services, and business models successfully. A serial entrepreneur, Mike has launched three successful businesses and chairs the Gathering of Titans entrepreneurial conclave at MIT. Mike is a featured columnist for *BloombergBusinessWeek.*

Luisa Uriarte is a partner and executive vice president of Maddock Douglas where she is the head of research. Luisa has more than 20 years of experience in managing research and consulting projects of international scope, covering more than 30 countries worldwide.

Javier Flaim, formerly an executive vice president at Maddock Douglas, is an expert at repositioning and launching new products and brands. Previously the CEO of Markitecture, a marketing research and innovation firm, Javi is a member of the Vocational Foundation, Inc., a non-profit organization dedicated to helping disadvantaged youth in the New York City area gain the skills they need to achieve financial independence.

Brett S. Miller, a vice president of innovation at Maddock Douglas, is a 20-year marketing veteran who has spearheaded domestic and international innovation initiatives for such clients as Allstate, Blue Cross Blue Shield, BP, Chase, GE, Jim Beam Brands, Kellogg's, KIA, Kohler, Kraft, LG, Levis, MetLife, Miller Brewing Company, Samsung, Starbucks, Toyota, Unilever, Wal-Mart, and Whirlpool.

A long-time contributor to *The New York Times*, **Paul B. Brown** is a former writer and editor for *Business Week, Financial World, Forbes*, and *Inc.* He is the author (or co-author) of numerous best-sellers, including *Customers for Life* written with Carl Sewell and *Your Marketing Sucks* with Mark Stevens. Paul is a contributing editor to both the MIT *Sloan Management Review* and *The Conference Board Review*.

Brand New

PART

I

PREPARATION AND STRATEGY

CHAPTER 1

The Innovation Paradox

The problem is simple, and indeed, paradoxical. Research shows people like new products and services. They want them. And, indeed, they go out of their way to try to find them. Yet companies are truly terrible at providing the new products and services that meet their customers' needs.

In the 1980s, research showed nine out of 10 new products failed. Some 30 years later, nothing has changed. Our research—confirmed by other firms—shows that nine out of 10 new products still fail today.

Moreover, when you look deeper—and we will walk you through our proprietary data in a minute—you actually find a second paradox within the original paradox: companies know introducing new products and services successfully is something they need to do to ensure a healthy future. And yet they readily concede that they are not devoting sufficient resources to make it happen. And at the risk of having this sound like the business equivalent of a matryoshka (those Russian dolls that nest inside one another) the reality is that there is even a third paradox within the second paradox within the initial paradox: Firms are aware that they have a problem—they openly admit that are not very good at introducing new products and services—but they have made remarkably little effort to improve their batting averages—apparently convinced that introducing new products is inherently a hit or miss process.

When you add all this up, it is easy to understand why there is a huge gap between customers' desires for new products and the ability for companies to deliver them. We call this the innovation paradox. And the situation is far worse than most senior managers and marketing executives believe.

A Look at the Numbers

Let's spend a couple of minutes and look at just how severe the problem is by reviewing the research we have at our fingertips. In 2004, 2008, and again in 2010, we surveyed a representative sample of the nation's best companies. In the first survey we talked to marketers at firms of all sizes. In the second survey we limited our questions to companies that are members of the Association of National Advertisers (an organization of some 300 companies of bigger firms with a total of more than 8,000 brands). And in the third, we went back out to a representative sample of the marketing decision makers. In all three instances, almost half the people we talked to were in senior positions like director of marketing or above. Here's what we found:

As the first line in Table 1.1 shows, about 80 percent of companies say their futures depend on introducing new products. That fact is not surprising. It is commonplace to hear a CEO say something like, "five years from now, we expect a third of our revenues to come from products that don't exist today."

And it is not just the CEO who is preaching about the importance of new products. Wall Street is as well. This excerpt from the *Harvard Business Review:*

> "Top-line revenue growth, especially organic growth, ultimately boosts shareholder value, so investors increasingly demand it. In fact, the presumption of organic growth is baked into companies' stock value. *If you decompose the stock prices of the leading consumer product companies, you'll see that future growth accounts for as much as 54% of the stock's value.*"[1]

---

[1]Harvard Business Review, November 2004.

Table 1.1 What Executives Think about Their New Product Prowess

How much do you agree or disagree with the following statements about new products or new services in business?	2004 (100) %	2008 ANA (118) %	2010 (152) %
I believe the future success of my company depends on our ability to successfully develop and introduce new products or services	78	87	80
Our company strategy calls for a steady flow of new products or new services	57	71	59
My company does not dedicate the full resources necessary to properly develop and launch new products or new services	31	53	42
We are working to be better at developing and launching new products or new services	85	84	78
Compared to 5 years ago, the investment needed to launch new products or services has significantly increased	52	70	51
We use outside resources to help us develop new products or services	46	58	40
My company really excels when it comes to developing new products or services and launching them successfully	39	32	39
We have a "new product/service development process" that is well integrated across the company departments	45	46	33
Compared to 5 years ago, we are no more efficient at new product/service marketing	15	17	31
We really don't look at new products or services as being worth the effort	4	3	5
New products or new services fail so often they are way too risky	10	3	4

We added the emphasis in italics. But there isn't a single senior manager we know who would disagree with this statement. You see proof of it in the second line of Table 1.1, where the majority of executives agree with the statement "our company strategy calls for a steady flow of new products." What should follow from lines one and two is that companies are pouring tons of money into the new product development process. But that is simply not the case in practice, as you can see from line three of Table 1.1. When asked if they agreed with the following statement: "my company does *not* dedicate the full resources necessary to properly develop and launch new products," more than half (53 percent) of ANA members agreed.

Theoretically, that wouldn't necessarily be a huge problem. If the cost of new product introductions were falling, then a lack of resources is something that could be overcome by having really smart people—those with extensive experience in handling new product introductions—work full-time on getting new products into the customers' hands. They'd come up with oodles of products, introduce them all into the marketplace, and something would be bound to resonate with consumers.

Theoretically that could work. But the reality is, as line four in Table 1.1 shows, the cost of new product introductions is going up, not down. The majority of people said the cost of new product introductions is higher than it was five years ago. So the "let's-try-everything-and-see-what-resonates" approach is not going to work. The fact that it is more and more expensive to introduce new products—meaning the cost of new product failure is also climbing—is daunting. And the situation gets even more disheartening when we get to the question of expertise.

> The cost of new product introductions climbs steadily higher. That makes bungling an introduction not only embarrassing—but increasingly expensive.

Companies understand what follows from all this and you see the depressing results in line seven: only about a third of executives believe their company "excels" at introducing new products. But, there is hope in that at least half of the people surveyed understand one of their problems in bringing new products successfully to market: They don't have a fully integrated process for doing so.

They have a process for evaluating acquisitions. They have a process for reviewing people for raises and promotions. They even have a process for ordering paper clips, yet, as line seven in Table 1.1 tells us, they don't have a process for something that is vital to their company's future—handling new product introductions.

And Then It Really Falls Apart

What is *seemingly* clear from everything we have just talked about is that companies recognize that they need to introduce new products successfully. And yet at the same time they concede that they are not as good at the process of introducing new products as they should be. But we say "seemingly" because of the way the executives answered the questions in Table 1.1.

The Executive's Reactions

The overwhelmingly positive response to the question "we are working to be better at developing and launching new products," can be read two ways. Everybody says they're doing that but it also could just be an acknowledgment that senior executives recognize that they have a problem when it comes to new product introductions and they are taking steps to improve the people and processes required to increase their success rate. It *could* be read that way. But, it also could be whistling past the graveyard. Who wants to admit publicly that they have a problem and aren't doing anything about it? Of course you are going to say that you are working on fixing a problem—even if you are not really doing very much at all.

And spending an extra minute with the numbers confirms the whistling past the graveyard theory. Executives concede they don't have a well integrated "new product/service development process and admit they do "not dedicate the full resources necessary to properly develop and launch new products or new services."

By inference, line 11 supports the whistling past the graveyard theory. Senior executives know they are not good at introducing new products (line seven), and they told us that a key reason for that is that the people they rely on to introduce the new products—brand and product managers—don't have the requisite skill (line five). And yet, in 2010, only four in 10 companies brought in outside resources to help.

Executives are saying, in essence, "we are going to continue to work on new products ourselves—even though:

a.   we know we are not very good at it, (and as we discuss later in this chapter, the "we" includes marketers themselves);

b.   we have a terrible track record when it comes to introducing new products successfully, and;

c.   we really don't have a clue what the problem is so that we can improve our performance."

To be kind, the executives' reactions do not make sense. Can you imagine any CEO (who wants to keep his job) saying these sorts of things when it comes to business process improvement; or how the finance department should be run; or how they should go about hiring better employees? They wouldn't dare to . . . so why should new product introductions be any different?

Marketers: One of the Enemies Within

In further looking at the numbers, we noticed marketers poorly graded their company's ability to introduce new products. That got us to wondering how good they thought *they themselves* were at it. Their answer: not very.

We surveyed marketers from the same two groups we talked about earlier and said, "please rate yourself in these three main actions associated with new product marketing:

- Introducing new products;
- Developing and introducing line extensions;
- And repositioning or relaunching a product."

We asked them to give themselves an A if they were extremely good at an activity; a B if they were good; a C if they thought they were average; a D if they thought they were poor at something; and an F if they flat out stunk in a particular category. Table 1.2 shows how they responded.

As you can see, the vast majority of marketers gave themselves extremely low marks. For example, if you look at the first column—introducing new products—you see that less than half of the respondents (49 percent) gave themselves an A or B. In the third column—introducing products into new channels or markets—the scores were just as bad.

In fact, the second column—introducing line or brand extensions—is the only place where there were more As and Bs than there were Cs, Ds, and Fs and it wasn't by much—just 52 percent gave themselves good marks.

Where Do We Go from Here?

So where do these numbers leave us? What do they all mean? Well, for one thing, they mean the New Product Paradox we described at the beginning of this chapter is real. Customers want new products, and many companies

Table 1.2 Grading of Strategy, Planning, and Execution

Overall, how would you grade your company's success in terms of the results of these initiatives?	% Among those who gave their company a grade of "A" or "B" (i.e., Top 2 Box)		
	2004 (100) %	2008 ANA (118) %	2010 (152) %
Line or brand extensions	66	57	52
Totally new product or services	62	43	49
Re-positioning or re-launching existing products or services	63	39	49
New channels and/or markets	55	30	42

are extremely bad at providing them. But we also know something else from the survey results. Companies are just starting to say—reluctantly—in public that they have a problem and are committed to solving it.

Jeffery Immelt, chairman and CEO of GE, in a recent address to shareholders, talked about the need for an "innovation imperative" at his company, whose stock has been essentially flat for years. Steve Ballmer, CEO of Microsoft, said in a recent interview that he believes innovation is the only way his company can satisfy customers and stay ahead of the competition. And William Ford, Jr., chairman of Ford Motor Co., says that from now on, innovation will be the compass by which his company sets its strategy.

Creating new products and services will be at the heart of those innovation initiatives and that, of course, takes us full circle: people want new products and services, and companies want to do a better job of providing them. The problem is they don't know how. And that is where we come in.

> People want new products and services, and companies want to do a better job of providing them. That makes the New Product Paradox that much more frustrating.

A Unique Process

Before we start talking about how to solve the new product paradox, you might have a few questions about who we are and why you should believe us.

Our experience as part of Maddock Douglas (the mind-to-market innovation agency that exists to bring industry-changing ideas to market) positions us perfectly to give you the freshest perspectives on rethinking how companies create anything new. In fact, 25 percent of Fortune 100 companies, and scores of small and entrepreneurial firms, have turned to us to help them identify the biggest unmet needs in their industry, brainstorm game-changing new products and services and business models that address these needs, then brand and launch the best ideas into the market. Solving the new product paradox is the part of the business world we have devoted our lives to and, because of this, we have noticed one thing over and over again: There is a root cause for the failures of almost all new product introductions and it is that, *invariably, companies do not have a disciplined, replicable process that employs a mix of creativity and science to introduce new products efficiently and effectively.*

Intuitively, most of us could probably list the individual components that need to be included in such a process. For example, they would include:

- A dedicated "new product" team.
- A marketing-driven orientation within the firm (i.e., senior leadership at the company would identify a customer need in the marketplace and set out to fill it, as opposed to having finance, R&D (research and development), or some other function to come up with an idea and see if anyone was interested.
- Dedicated financial resources.
- Constant testing and re-forecasting before launch.
- Recognition that there is no "first-mover" advantage (so it is far better to get the product right than to be first in the marketplace).

The questions then remain: how do you tie all these elements together into a new product strategy, and how do you implement and execute the strategy you've developed? Answering these two questions makes up the heart of solving the innovation paradox.

> Companies need a disciplined, replicable process that employs a mix of creativity and science to introduce new products efficiently and effectively. We are going to give it to you.

The Brand New Strategy

After more than 20 years working with hundreds of clients and interviewing literally thousands of marketing executives we have developed an over-arching strategy we call Brand New. It is a strategy specifically focused on how to create and introduce new products effectively—and with a far greater rate of success.

Phase 1: Need

There is a natural tendency to want to start with THE BIG IDEA. That is understandable but wrong. The place to begin is to find the needs/opportunity in the marketplace. But all needs are not created equal. They need to be rank ordered not only by size, but also by your organization's ability to fill them.

Phase 2: Idea

Having identified the need, you come up with literally hundreds of ideas—including business models—that might work. Then the best ideas are refined and optimized using quantitative research to determine which concepts—and in which form—have the greatest chance of being a hit with customers. Here you are looking to discover the precise attributes consumers are looking for in terms of your potential concept's design, price, packaging, and features.

Phase 3: Communication/Commercialization

This is, we have found, the most overlooked piece of the innovation process. Stellar communication links the idea to the need in the customers/consumers mind and an organization's ability to *make money* and have the innovation become a viable commercial success. It's what gets them to say, "You listened to me and I'll pay you for coming up with what I told you I wanted.

Execution

Now, it is one thing to have a well-defined process for introducing new products efficiently; it is quite another to make that process a reality. Far too often it is the inability to execute the new product strategy that leads to a worthy product failing in the marketplace. To make sure that does not happen, we will spend a substantial amount of time in this book explaining how you can execute your strategy. But let us make one brief point here: a key part of your implementation plan should call for the creation of interdisciplinary teams that work together to make a new product idea a successful reality.

One of the major reasons new products fail is that individual departments work in a vacuum or silo, having little if any interaction with the overall new product development process and it simply does not work. For example, on its own, an R&D department has no mechanism for discovering what the market wants. It can come up with incredibly cool products, but that doesn't do the company any good unless the products satisfy a consumer need. As you will see, our process calls for all the departments within a company to work together.

By tying all the departments together during the new product development process (which we will show you how to do in the pages that follow) you greatly increase your chances of coming up with a product that customers want. The net result: It becomes easier (and less costly) to bring to market new products and services that have a far greater chance of gaining acceptance in the marketplace.

> It's a perfect inverse ratio: The more silos, the less chance you have for innovation success.

You Must Remember This

1. **It's a process.** Innovation, just like any other part of your business can be managed effectively. In fact, it must be. A failed innovation is both embarrassing and expensive.
2. **Begin with the need.** The world's landfills are cluttered with really cool ideas ... that no one wanted.
3. **Break down the walls.** The more handoffs (or walls) between departments the greater the chance that your innovation effort will fail.

Coming Up Next

You wouldn't think of introducing an inventory management system at random, or wait for inspiration to strike before ordering office supplies. Why then would you leave the way you introduce new products or services up to chance?

In the pages ahead, we will provide you with a detailed process to use to efficiently introduce new products time after time.

Let's begin.

2

Creating an Efficient and Effective Innovation Process

Every year, hundreds of millions of dollars—and thousands of jobs—are lost in what we call "the innovation abyss," the place where seemingly promising new ideas go to their justifiable deaths.

While some companies have mastered nailing the right insight and consistently delivering evolutionary or revolutionary ideas against it—and create the 10 percent of new products that actually succeed—others spend their time creating new products and services that are at best irrelevant and expensive—and career ending.

If you find yourself struggling with your innovation efforts from time to time, you are probably tempted to ask, "what gives?" The answer—which we've learned by working with hundreds of clients over the last 20 years—is relatively easy to explain.

In this chapter, we will detail how industry-changing ideas and products are delivered into the marketplace. Simply put, the companies and marketers we see thrashing about don't fully understand how cost effective innovation occurs. And even those who have had some success are usually starting in the wrong place and would be more successful—and far more profitable—if they modified their approach. The fact is, there is a proven method to safely and consistently deliver game-changing ideas. But it dosen't begin where you think.

The Big Three: How Does Industry-Changing Innovation Happen?

Innovation occurs at the synchronized intersection of:

1. A meaningful insight or market need;
2. A new product, service, or business model that meets that need, and;
3. Communication that connects the two.

While the three interlocking rings in Figure 2.1 show you exactly where innovation occurs (you can see it in the middle represented by "MD"), there's another way to think about it, one that could explain why you might be having trouble introducing new products and/or services successfully.

Think of our definition of innovation as a three-legged stool. Most companies successfully build only one or two of the legs, causing their innovation efforts to topple and fail. You need all three legs, or pillars (if you prefer a building metaphor) to be successful. And you will be a lot more successful, and waste far less money, if you take the right steps in the right order.

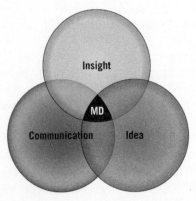

Figure 2.1   **Where Innovation Happens**

Determining the Need to Formulate the Idea

We know that including all three pillars as a part of their brainstorming is *not* what most companies do. They usually start first with a really cool idea for a product or service idea. For instance, somebody in research and development (R&D) develops a cell phone that will allow you to make calls from the top of Mount Kilimanjaro to anywhere in the world; or a bunch of really smart people sit in a room and decide "what this new Internet thing needs is its own online currency" that can serve as an alternative to credit cards; or someone in the company says, "I have the perfect solution to the fact that there are too many cars on the road, and people are too lazy to walk short distances or take a bike. Why don't we create a two-wheel motorized scooter?"

In these examples, what resulted from these product ideas were (in order): the Iridium phone, Flooz currency, and the Segway. In each case the product did exactly what it was designed to do. But, in terms of our three-legged model, there wasn't a very large need. Not enough people cared. (Oceans of red ink, and pink slips by the ream, followed shortly thereafter.) That's why you want to start by devoting a disproportionate amount of your time to discovering the market need.

Now, if you think you already have The Greatest Idea Ever, by all means test it. Ask if people want to be able to call anywhere at any time (just about everyone would say yes) then tell them what it would cost not only for the phone (a lot) but per minute (yikes!) and then see if your potential market still thinks your new product is a good idea. It's okay if they don't. It sounds strange, but failure is a key part of innovating efficiently. You just don't want those failures to cost you a fortune (more on this later).

It sounds strange, but failure is a key part of innovation.

The best way to develop your new product, service or business model efficiently is by figuring out what the market needs and, more specifically, what the market needs that they would readily accept coming from you, your brand, or a company you could acquire. We will be talking about how you determine that need in Chapter 3. But we also suggest you do more: We will recommend that you infuse outside experts in all of these well-tested methodologies. Ask them to be part of the customer interactions, the data review, and the insight development. They will help you see things that your expertise keeps you from seeing and they will help you come up with even more needs than you would on your own, and this is a good thing. In fact, we've literally increased insights ten-fold by adding outside experts to traditional processes. We know larger quantities of insights increases the likelihood of breakthrough ideas.

Now, take the most compelling insights and quantitatively test them to see which ones your customers tell you are the most valuable. While your favorite insight may not make the cut here, you want to fish where the most fish are, so it is important that you leave your ego aside and focus your team on developing products against the needs that rank highest. The process that you go through will be eye-opening and valuable in terms of discovering insights through both successes and failures.

Small Disasters Welcome   Failure isn't fatal. In fact, as we said earlier, failure is actually a requirement for innovation success. Common sense tells you the odds are ridiculously small that you are going to get your new product or service absolutely right the first time so, in order to make your new idea everything it can be, it needs to be repeatedly soft-launched with both internal stakeholders and external customers, with the understanding that it will be modified (perhaps extensively) based on how they react.

This means you are going to fail—maybe a lot—before you get it right. You need to accept this fact if you are going to do your best work. And it is a concept you must get across to your team—and indeed your entire company—in order to free it from the innovation-limiting shackles of trying to be perfect from the start.

For successful launches to happen, everyone must be okay with the premise you are starting with what some may consider a half-baked idea and that the concept may very well fail as initially constituted. That's fine. You need to tell your team that the real failure is the fear of launching an idea before it is perfect because, by then, the need you have identified may have been filled by someone else, or morphed into something new.

> Don't wait to launch an idea until it is perfect.

To buttress your case that failure is okay, make the following points:

1. Nothing happens until the customer says "yes." We think we have a great idea, but the people who pay us (our customers) will tell us if it's actually true or we need to change it.
2. We can make changes quickly and cheaply. It's possible to simulate years of research data in just months once we are out in the marketplace. The Internet can give us instant feedback; empty strip malls allow for in-and-out shopping experiences with risk-free short-term leases; technology has made prototyping doable in days instead of weeks. In short, it has never been cheaper to test ideas.
3. It won't hurt much. We will be making our "mistakes" on a small scale—that is, we won't be launching the Iridium

Phone or Segway only to find no one understands it or only 1,000 people want it. If we find out our idea is completely off base, we'll save the organization a fortune (not to mention our jobs).

Translating the Idea to the Market

Now that you understand failure is part of the innovation process, one of the questions we always ask when people complain to us that their hot new innovation effort has yet to gain traction is this: "Do customers understand how it will make their life better and/or easier?" Invariably we hear some variation from innovators of, "how could they not?" Our response is always: "Let's stop for a minute and make sure that is true," and we give them a couple of analogies to underscore our point.

You know that feeling you get in your gut when your IT department explains—using industry shorthand—a cool new technology? Think. What percentage of those words do you understand? It can mirror how you felt on your first day in chemistry class, when you were being passionately taught something that had no relevance to you at all. What if this is how you are making your customers feel? What if they don't understand your new product? What if the words you are using to describe its usefulness don't resonate with them? What if they don't see the benefits?

To make sure your message is clear, here's a suggestion: Hire an interpreter. This method of bridging the gap is an example of "insight work." The insight work you do up front isn't just about finding the need, it's about hearing—*really hearing*—how your customers talk about it, and from our experience you won't be able to do this alone. Your expert brain will subconsciously interpret their wishes using your own language (i.e., "of course I heard him. He said he needed whole life insurance") but involving communication experts as part of your insight work will allow them (an independent party) to translate the needs for you, using the customer's language, not yours. In turn, the independent party will make sure the way in which you describe your offering will be clear to your target audience.

Throughout the book we are going to talk about how to infuse outside experts into your innovation process. It's a great way to gain different perspectives and help you stay on track. We believe the important step of finding independent input to describe your offering is intuitively obvious. But what we are going to talk about next is not.

Selling the Idea   As you set off to create a product or service to fill the market need you have discovered, be careful to avoid the place where companies often stumble. Many times innovators get greedy and try to have their product or service appeal to too wide an audience. Of course you want to maximize revenues but if you try to have your product do too much—or appeal to too many people—you run the very real risk of confusing your potential market and have sales fall far short of where you intended.

TiVo serves as a case in point. We are convinced that one reason it took so long to catch on—and as a result of which is that it is now seen as just another form of digital video recorder (DVR)—is that the company was never clear about which need it was meeting.

The challenge for TiVo, like many other innovative products or services, is that it is capable of meeting many different kinds of needs. It can record whatever show you want it to, so it replaces your VCR. It can anticipate and find shows that you may be interested in watching, so it replaces your best friend's recommendations. It allows you to skip over commercials, so it makes television watching more efficient—you can watch an hour-long program in about 45 minutes—giving you more time to do other things. These are just a few of the many, many benefits of owning a TiVo and they all sound great; maybe too great. For the longest time, the company seemed to try to promote all these features—presumably to appeal to as many people as possible—and they wound up confusing the masses. By the time TiVo discovered that perhaps its strongest selling feature was that it was easier to use than a VCR, it was already out in the marketplace and the delay in streamlining its benefits had squandered tremendous momentum. By quantifying insights before going to market they would have been able to avoid this costly, and common, error. If they had better communicated and focused on the single insight/need that consumers said they liked most—and let the market discover all of the other benefits on its own—TiVo, a great product, would likely have dominated the market from the start.

> Make sure you communicate the strongest feature of your new product to the customer. And only that strongest feature. Focus, focus, focus.

The point is, not only do you have to create a product or service that meets the marketplace need you have pinpointed, you must also make sure that the potential customers understand that is what you have done. That, of course, brings us to the third and final part of the innovation process.

Sending a Clear Message

We mean this with all sincerity: The insurance industry is one of the most innovative industries we know of. Your first reaction may be, "huh?" or, "you must be kidding?" and that underscores that insurers haven't mastered the art of effectively telling the world how they have created products and services to meet its needs. But the fact remains, however, that the insurance industry is remarkably innovative. You want to figure out a way to leave money to your heirs—when you don't have a lot—or replace the annual pension your company has eliminated, or induce a really smart business person to join your board (when they are petrified *they* will be sued if *you* make a dumb decision)? The insurance industry has a product for each scenario. (Life insurance, immediate annuities, and officers and directors insurance, respectively.) And there are countless other examples (appliance insurance; health insurance; key person insurance, mortgage insurance. . .) of how the industry solves the very specific needs of its potential clients.

Unfortunately, the fact that insurers aren't very good at communicating that they have the perfect product for any number of needs, unfortunately, is not unusual. Many times the best insights and products are overwhelmed in the marketplace by poorly executed communication. From our experience the more established, conservative, and profitable the industry, the more likely it is to face this challenge.

What can you do to avoid a fate similar to that of the insurance industry? These three ideas will help:

1. *Press 1 for English.* Do you know what "Universal Life," "Variable Life," or "Whole Life" are? Don't be embarrassed if you don't. Like most industries, insurance often forgets that its professionals are the only ones who understand its language. This is a huge mistake that too many of us make. You want to talk to your customers using the words and terms they do in describing your offering. If you don't, you are making your job 50 times harder than it has to be.

2. *Get the Benefit Right.* This is similar to the TiVo problem. TiVo couldn't figure out what benefit to stress. The insurance industry can't decide how to describe it. They aren't selling "life insurance," they are selling "making sure your spouse is taken care of and the kids can go to college protection." When companies connect the correct insight/benefit to the product and communicate the benefit evocatively, something magical happens. It sells.

3. *Engage the Influencers.* Now more than ever, social media sites allow us to find those who really care the most and get them engaged with our new idea. We can ask for their insights about how to communicate it, and give them credit. Make them evangelists and carriers of the message. Once your campaign starts, they will be invested in it and help propel it. In the case of insurance what kind of influencers are we talking about: well, insurance agents, of course, but also CPAs, attorneys, bankers, and financial planners; all the people we turn to when we have financial questions.

Innovating successfully is hard enough without getting in our own way. Following in order, the three steps we have talked about will make innovating more efficient (meaning, less costly) and far less frustrating.

You Must Remember This

1. **Ad libbing is costly.** To innovate efficiently and effectively, follow the steps in order. First, identify the market need, then create a product or service to fill it, and finally, make sure you communicate clearly what you have come up with.
2. **Each step in the innovation process is equally important.** There are no shortcuts. If you short-change one, your efforts will invariably fail.
3. **If the customers don't understand what you have.** It is your fault, not theirs.

Coming Up Next

Because need/insight, idea, and the communication that links the two are so important, we will be devoting the next three chapters to them. We will begin with how you can discover a huge need in the marketplace.

3

Circle #1: Finding the Need

Almost everyone thinks successful innovation starts with a great idea. Almost everyone is wrong. The great idea comes second. You must begin with the killer insight.

Why is finding the insight the starting point? That's simple. Ideas are easy. It's the insight that is hard—but vitally important.

We think that big beautiful ideas are a dime a dozen. Want proof? Okay.

Perhaps you are reading this during lunch. Hmmm, let's see. Lunch related ideas. Why doesn't my sandwich container lock snuggly next to my snack container, which fits correctly into a bag or briefcase? That way, I would always remember to pack everything for me or my kids. And why hasn't someone designed a system to arrange all of the miscellaneous storage containers and lids in a drawer at home so it will actually close and I can easily find the matching lid? Speaking of lids, why are they not color coded to help me find the matching container? Or, why don't container companies just fiddle with the depth so all the lids fit on the same size container–like fast food beverage cups?

Does it even have to have a separate lid? Couldn't it be built into the unit?

And while we are on the subject, why hasn't someone invented a washable version of the zipper seal bag? I could fold it, reuse it, and store it more easily. It could use origami thinking–like a Chinese takeout container–so it was rigid, foldable, and sealable!

You get the picture. Coming up with ideas isn't a problem. But, ironically, starting with the idea can be.

Insight First, Idea Second

Let's say you leave work early on Friday, just after finishing lunch you brought in those nifty containers we just talked about and head immediately to your home away from home: a house you have on a lake. You love it. You go there every weekend. But you wish the nearby town wasn't so sleepy and down at its heels. To improve the place, you and a bunch of your friends get together and brainstorm ideas. For instance, saying "the restaurants downtown are great, but we need to find other things for adults to do," shoots you off in one direction. Improvements might then include a regional theater, a movie house that shows foreign films, more boutique shops. But if you begin by saying "downtown is boring. There is nothing for the kids to do," you go off in an entirely different direction with improvements like carnivals or water parks or amusement parks like LegoLand, and so on.

Either course of action would be perfectly valid, if the need is big enough. If it is not, you would find yourself in a lot of trouble. For example, there may absolutely be a need for more things for adults to do downtown, but five miles away (in a neighboring town) there are more activities for adults (including a local branch of the state university and all its related concerts, art shows, and lectures, etc.) than you could do in a month of weekends. And yes, there is no doubt it would be helpful if there were more kids' activities. But, there are serious doubts about whether this particular lake community, created on the Club Med model, is ever going to be seen as "kid friendly." Remember when Las Vegas tried to advertise it was the perfect place for a family vacation? Hundreds of millions of dollars later they discovered no one believed them. That's why they are back to "what happens in Vegas, stays in Vegas."

The point is, the place to start the innovation process is by coming up with an insight into a huge problem waiting to be solved. That's what we are going to do here. This chapter walks you through exactly the same process we have developed and tweaked over many years of experience that has helped companies such as Allstate, Blue Cross Blue Shield, Heinz, Kellogg's, Kraft, Miller, P&G, Toyota, and Whirlpool (to name a few) discover marketplace needs.

Taking a Step Back

Before you can start looking for an insight, you need to know what an insight is. An insight, for the purposes of innovation, must be a penetrating customer truth rich enough to generate significant ideas that can help build your business. It must be penetrating in that it needs to be true for a large group of people. If it is not, then your potential business opportunity is limited. In other words, if you cannot drive business with it, it's not an insight. It's trivia. This is the big leagues. Trivia is unacceptable. If that's all you have, try again.

> Ultimately, an insight seeks to make someone's life simpler, more convenient, and more economical; perhaps even more worthwhile.

How do you know when you're on to something? Compare your insight against these three criteria:

1. You can express the insight in terms of a statement of facts from the customer's point of view.
2. There are clear reasons why the facts are true.

3. But there is a problem, or tension, in the marketplace that needs resolution before you can give people what they want.

If there is nothing to solve for, you may have found something that is true but it is not an insight. For example, "I like to eat fast food because I can get in and out of the restaurant quickly" is clearly a statement that satisfies the first two conditions. There is a statement of fact ("I like to eat fast food") and we know why the fact is true ("because I can get out of the restaurant quickly.") But there is no tension. There is nothing to solve for. Fast food restaurants are abundant, and no one is really clamoring for fast food to be served faster.

The same sort of situation exists if someone tells you, "I like to fly when I have a meeting that is more than 300 miles away. It's faster." Again, we have the statement of fact and the reason why, but no tension.

Having a tension does two things. First, it keeps you focused. There is clarity. You know what you are solving for. Second, it makes communication (see Chapter 5) substantially easier since you know what you want to talk to the customer about. So if you want to reduce searching for an insight to a formula, it would look like this:

I (insert "fact" here) because (insert "why" here) but (insert "tension" here).

For example:

I use storage containers for lunch because it cuts down on waste but I can never find the matching lids.

Finding the Tension

By finding the tension, you are solving for the pain. Another way to look at it is that you are solving for the "but." (Invariably, when we put it like this during a workshop, someone says, "so what we are really trying to do is eliminate the pain in the butt." Or worse, someone says, "you mean our goal at today's workshop is to find the biggest "buts"? In either case, we always grimace—and then agree.)

You can see the difference between "I like to eat fast food because I can get in and out of the restaurant quickly," and "I like to eat fast food, because I can get out of the restaurant quickly, but two hours later I don't feel so well because they don't always uses the best ingredients." Similarly, there is a striking difference between, "I like to fly when I have a meeting that is more than 300 miles away. It's faster," and, "I like to fly when I have a meeting that is more than 300 miles away because it's faster, but the security lines are incredibly frustrating." In the latter cases, you now have something to solve for. (Better tasting fast food, for example, or creating things for people to do while they are waiting in security lines.)

One more example to hammer home the point: For a pet food company, the insight could flow from talking to a dog owner who says, "I really love to feed Barky scraps from the dinner table, because it makes him so happy. But I know people food doesn't necessarily have the nutrition he needs." The tension here could lead to a new line of dog food treats marketed this way: "You're having spaghetti and meatballs for dinner? Give your dog *Love Your Pet*'s spaghetti-and-meatball-flavored treats, shaped like the real thing and containing one hundred percent of the vitamins he needs."

This new product flows logically from our insight formula:

- We had the facts from the customer's point of view: "I really love to feed Barky scraps from the dinner table."
- We had a clear reason why those facts are true: "I feed Barky scraps because it 'makes him so happy.'"
- But there is a problem: People food is not necessarily nutritious for dogs.

The key in every case is to pay special attention to the tension, the thing keeping the customer from getting their needs met.

> If your solution is not addressing an unmet need in the marketplace, it is not an insight. (And if you don't have an insight, you won't have an innovation.)

Narrowing Your Focus: Segmentation

If you think about it, there are two key parts of the first (insight) circle:

1. Who you target, and
2. What are their unmet needs (i.e., what are you solving for).

Looked at in that way, you have a huge potential opportunity—too huge as it turns out. There are more than 6.8 billion people in the world and each one of them has a virtually unlimited number of potential needs. You need some way of segmenting your potential audience.

You already know there are millions of ways to segment a market. For example, you can do it by:

- Demographics (age, income, region)
- Corporgraphics (size of company, SIC code, region, revenue)
- By zip code
- By attitudes/interest
- What they read. For example, tell us what magazine is on your coffee table, and chances are we can tell you a lot about who you are/what you do/what your interests are.

All this, and the other segmentation types you are familiar with are fine—and can be useful later, but they are *not* your starting point in trying to figure out who to go after.

You need to employ a simple three-part formula: define success, define the characteristics you want your segment to have, and then find what predicts/correlates with these variables. Let's run through the steps one at a time.

Step 1. Define Success

Here you want to be as specific as possible. For example, you might say:

- We want to create $100 million in incremental revenue in 24 months.
- It must leverage our core competencies in manufacturing.
- It must be branded under our name.
- It must be patented and protected.

In other words, you are trying to make sure that in addition to bringing in revenues, the new product/service you are going to add fits with what your company does for a living.

Step 2. Define the Characteristics You Want Your Segment to Have

For example, you want your potential customers to be:

- Growing—the last thing you want to do is target a segment that is decreasing in number.
- Spending—you don't want to go after a group that is *not* going to open its checkbook.
- Open to your brand—if they are perfectly happy with what they have, and can't imagine going with anyone else, all you are going to do—should you target them—is end up beating your head against a wall.

- Findable/reachable—it is lovely that you believe you want to sell to 43-year-old women who have a Ph.D. in microbiology, two kids, two dogs, a cat, and a hamster, and who live in the Midwest with their carpenter husbands. But finding such people is going to be extremely difficult.
- Decision makers—you want your target to make the buying decision on their own (or at least be able to answer honestly that they have 50%, or more, of the ability to make a purchasing decision).

Step 3. "Simply" Find What Predicts/Correlates with these Variables

Having decided who you want to target, you go and find the variables that will lead you to these people. An example will show you how all this plays out: Say you are a huge soft drink company and you are looking to create a $100 million brand that will fit with what you already have. You have just completed Step 1; you have defined what success will look like.

You want your potential customers to like (or at least be neutral about) your brand. If they say "I am never going to buy something from the makers of Brand X, then you don't want them. You want customers who are open to the idea of an additional kind of beverage coming from you and who will also be willing to try it.

Only then do you ask them what kind of drink they are looking for. Again, for Step 2, you are not going into this with any preconceived notion, you are solving for their need.

Well, it turns out that the biggest need you discover is that there is a large chunk of the market that wants an energy drink without caffeine. Customers want something that will give them a boost in the latter part of the day without affecting their sleep.

Having identified this market, you go out and ask potential customers within this market as many questions as you can possibly think of. Everything from how much the person weighs and what snacks they eat to whether they have kids or a pet.

Then you sort through the data and look for commonalities. This is Step 3.

In our hypothetical case, it looks like the people we should go after live in cities and have neither kids nor pets. Armed with this information, we look for the easiest way of targeting this segment. (See Figure 3.1.)

Now it is possible that your definition of success is so specific that your segmentation strategy will leap off the page: We want as many upscale (household income greater than $100,000) grandmothers as possible purchasing our product for girls, under the age of five, who are near and dear to them.

But most of the time we just don't have that kind of market need in mind and that's why you need to go through this three-step process.

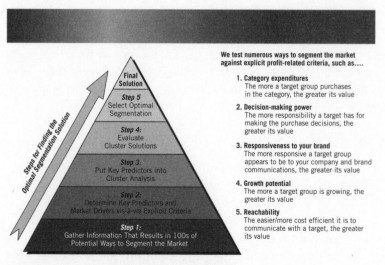

Figure 3.1   Steps for Optimal Segmentation Solutions

Most people do *not* do their segmentation this way. Why? Because it is easier to:

- Pick one variable (i.e., segment by age).
- Buy media. (Your product appeals to teenage girls? You place ads in *Seventeen* magazine.)
- Explain to your boss.

The problem with the "easy" approach is that it is not all that effective. Not only may you be overlooking one (or more) potential markets for your product or service, odds are you are going to be running into your competitors at every turn. (They, too, are likely to opt for the "easy," segment-by-one-variable method.)

If you don't segment smartly, just about all of your innovation efforts will be wasted. Your insights will be based on the wrong target. Your ideas will be based on the wrong customer mind-set and your communication will target the wrong individuals.

Segmentation is the place where all successful innovation efforts begin. That's why you need to let your goals and the data tell you how to target customers. It may be by zip code, the magazines they read, attitudes, or something else entirely. You simply don't know until you go through the three-step process.

What This Could Look Like

The outcome of your segmentation should look something like this. You decide you want to find:

- A target population that represents, for example, 20% of the market but 50% or *more* of the potential *future* economic value for your company or brand. As you see from the right hand side of Figure 3.2, that would

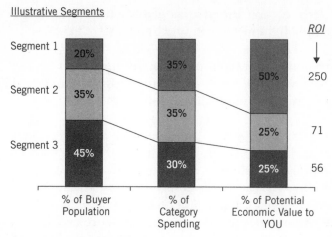

Figure 3.2   Segmentation Outcomes

generate a return of $2.50 for every marketing dollar you invest. Conversely, going after the least productive segment of the market would give you 56 cents back on every dollar you spend—you'd lose a lot of money.

- A segmentation that is *uniquely yours*, meaning:
  - It is not commonplace(i.e., you are not segmenting by zip code).
  - It is not something your competitors are using.
  - It is a proprietary segmentation that is yours and typically valid for several years of innovation effort.

We have people at Maddock Douglas who have been involved with successful segmentations for clients such as AT&T, Burberry, Coca-Cola, ExxonMobil, GE, Prudential, and Wells Fargo (to name just a few) that has led to *billions* of dollars (not a typo) of successful in-market innovation launches, using the segmentation model we just described.

Let's see how the process played out for one of our clients: the Million Dollar Round Table (MDRT).

The MDRT is a premier association of 30,000 financial professionals in 80 countries around the globe.

Yet despite their success, their president John Prast knew the organization was facing serious problems:

- U.S. membership was flat and declining–mirroring the trends of the U.S. insurance industry agent network as a whole.
- Renewal rates were at historic lows.
- The age of the member base was increasing fast.
- Attendance at their annual signature event was lower than ever.

MDRT was at a critical juncture. "We had to do something dramatic to turn things around," Prast told us. "We could hang our heads and blame the economy, and the changing nature of the industry. Or we could look at all the problems as a chance to reinvent ourselves."

Prast, with our help, began by segmenting the market. Following our three-step formula, he began by defining success. "We want to reach the people who will make us a relevant association for the next 100 years."

Specifically that meant three things:

1. Finding high-producing, younger members (so that they could be part of the association for decades to come).
2. Determining what new product offering the association should add to attract these new members (without alienating the existing base).
3. Creating a value proposition for all to rally around.

The main question was: did this younger, high-performing segment exist? The answer was yes. It turns out there were tens of thousands of them, all under the age of 40, who were looking for ways to grow their business. We dubbed these very successful professionals in the financial services industry "the young lions." MDRT would be a perfect match for them. The association could offer them business education, sales ideas, development of formal/informal partnerships, and networking/connecting with the "best of the best." And MDRT was well suited to deliver on all/most of their needs, it just had to develop and enhance many of the products and services they had traditionally offered.

We had found a segment that was definable and easy to reach. Finding people—even successful people who work in the financial services industry is relatively simple thanks to all the trade associations and industry directories.

Discovering and successfully attracting the young lions has reinvigorated MDRT and created a robust innovation pipeline of new services that will carry the organization well through the first half of the 21st Century.

As John said, "We have absolutely no intention of being complacent, but we couldn't be happier about where we are today."

One Final Segmentation Idea

There is one last point about this. There is significant power in deciding what channels you are going to use to segment your audience. For instance, have you thought about segmenting your sales channel (e.g., by brokers, dealers, and agents if you are in the insurance field, for example.) Or, if you're a consumer packaged goods company, what retail stores do you want to carry your product? You can even segment the staff within the stores where you sell your product. (Think "geniuses" in the Apple store, or the carpet specialist within a flooring store.) You get the point. You can use the power of segmentation to segment up and down the value chain to help identify open areas of opportunity.

Be Insight Agnostic

Once you know the framework to follow, the question becomes, "what is the best way to discover the insights themselves?" We're going to walk you through every step of the process but, before we do, we want to give you one key thought to keep in mind before you begin: **Be Insight Agnostic.**

This one is hard for the left-brainers. You've grown up with numbers. You love data, math, statistics, measurement, and charts. You get a secret thrill when the chief financial officer says, "prove it," because then it's about sizing the opportunity, quantifying the insight, modeling the return, and so on.

But there's a right time and a wrong time to require this level of quantification and the early stage of insight development is the wrong time. The truth is, insights can come from anywhere: a casual conversation with your friends, an article you read, a competitor's quote, your sales force, watching interactions with your customers, and talking with your colleagues about what you have observed in those interactions— or, sure, a large quantitative, statistically reliable, multiyear study of consumers and prospects. They *all* make for potentially fruitful areas for insight development. Be agnostic and let the sources of potential insights be vast and wide.

Insights by the Numbers

Yes, of course. Every insight you come across will not be valid. You also need to quantify the size of the insight to make sure you're headed in the right direction. Right now, though, you are looking for as many insights as you can get from every possible source. There are four steps toward discovering good insights:

- Having a target (know who you are trying to interest with your product or service);
- Observing that target;

- Reasoning together as a team (in a workshop, per-haps) to develop insights, and finally;
- Validating the insights the team discovers.

Let's take them one at a time.

Defining the Target The first thing you need is a clearly defined target. Who are you going after? Obviously, it can't be too broad a group otherwise your insights will get watered down as you try to reach the least common denominator.

If you have multiple or extremely large segments—all women, for example—you need to go through analyzing the needs for each one and, as you know, there are numerous way to sort. For example, even if you say you're going to target women ages 21 to 39, you need to be even more specific. Are those women living the *Sex and the City* lifestyle, or are they married? If they are married, do they have kids or not? If they have kids, how many? Do they live in the city, sub-urbs, or a rural area? Are the women in the suburbs who are married with kids adventurous, or reserved? You need to do this kind of targeting because what is true of one group—what your *Sex and the City* cohort likes to do on a Saturday night—does not always translate to other groups (such as reserved women who are married with kids.) Sometimes it does but you will not know until you go through this process for each.

> Before you can come up with a stellar insight, you need to generate hundreds of observations. And we mean that literally. You can't start with a list of 10; you need hundreds.

Observing the Target After you drill down on the target, you need to observe your target to start searching for needs. You can talk to them, of course. (One-on-one interviews, online surveys, focus groups, etc.) You can pull from personal experience—you are selling to teenagers and you have a couple of your own—or, you can read about the market and buy third-party research. The best solution, of course, is a combination of all of the above. But no matter how you do it, one thing is a must: observe the target in their environment, where they will use your product or service.

When it comes to in-environment observation, we like to have a team consisting of researchers, clients, and especially outside experts (more on this in Chapter 7) go into the field together. (You can do this with your staff alone, but the more eyes the better.) You should take this approach whether you are looking for an undiscovered need in the marketplace, or looking for ways to increase sales of an existing product or service. Invariably, you will discover things you could never have imagined. For example, a maker of a glass cleaner we worked with was amazed to learn that people were using it to clean surfaces of all sorts (which led them to modify their existing formula and create an entirely new second product, an all-purpose cleaner.) And by employing in-environment observation, you might suddenly understand why a product isn't selling.

We did some work for a maker of incontinence products for women who couldn't figure out why sales were so sluggish. There was clearly a need and the product performed superbly. By going out in the field, we realized that women would do anything possible to avoid buying the product in drug stores where it was on display with walkers, canes, and other products designed for the old. Not only did they have to pick up the product there, they then had to carry it to the register. We also suggested they offer customers to the opportunity to purchase the products by mail order and also told the firm to start seriously thinking about coming up with "designer" brands to eliminate the stigma.

Interpreting the Statements When you are out observing and talking to people, the statement of fact (i.e., "I really love feeding Barky scraps from the table") is very easy to gather. Most people can tell you the fact if you ask them. But, unfortunately, this step is not quite as simple as accurately writing down what people have to say. For one thing, not everyone is self-aware. For another, you want to pay attention to the non-verbal cues—the grunts, grimaces, and raised eyebrows.

Let's stay with dog food. When you ask someone about an "easy-open package" that contains the 25-pounds of *Retriever Mix* you sell—the one where your commercials show a four year old opening and closing the bag successfully—they might say, "it's fine," but their body language tells you it is anything but. In fact, when you probe a bit further, they might even tell you that invariably they end up tearing the bag, and a significant amount of that 25 pounds of dog food ends up on the floor. (They didn't want to tell you that because they did not want to seem less capable than a four year old.) In general, you want to look at what you see as well as hear and use your expertise, and that of others, to interpret it.

Here's another example. Invariably when you ask people about doing laundry they say, "it is no big deal." But when you watch them, you realize that may not be the case. They have to put the dirty clothes in a hamper, empty the hamper into a laundry basket, take the basket to the washing machine, sort the clothes by whites and colors, then put the white or color load into the washing machine (often bending over or reaching up to do so.) They then have to add soap and (perhaps) fabric softener, adjust the temperature settings, and turn on the machine.

Sounds like an ordeal to us. Could you make the process simpler? For example, could you create a detergent that could wash whites and colors at the same time (without turning the white sheets pink in the process)? Or could you manufacture a washing machine with a huge soap canister that would only have to be filled twice a year—think windshield fluid in your car—which would dispense the detergent automatically and alert you, via a warning light, when the machine was running low? These are all product ideas that could come out of your initial search for insights that consumers may never mention in a focus group.

As we said in the equation we offered earlier in this chapter—I (insert "fact" here) because (insert "why" here) but (insert "tension" here)—finding the "fact" portion of the equation is the most fairly straightforward. However, sometimes consumers can articulate the facts but many times they can't. This is where having multiple observers who can talk about what they have seen in a workshop could help enormously. We have found the most effective way to generate strong insights is in a workshop setting. But before we begin discussing how to conduct workshops, what happens there and why, here are three quick asides to keep in mind:

1. Collecting observations is a team sport and an important part of insight development. As a general rule whoever collected the observations should be in the workshop to help develop them (because you want the differing perspectives).

2. Before heading into any workshop, document the facts you have observed no matter how miniscule they seem and even if they were not expressed verbally. ("I saw Nancy struggle when she tried to open the bag of dog food." "Bill squinted when he tried to read the washing directions on our clothing prototype.")

3. Don't jump to conclusions. One observation does not make for an insight. Just like one focus group does not lead you to kill a product or an ad campaign . . . (at least, it shouldn't).

> We have found the most effective way to generate strong insights is in a workshop setting.

Workshops

A workshop should be conducted after the initial observations of a target are made. The good news is that everyone gathered in the room for the workshop has made observations about the target market. The bad news is that everyone has probably gone about it differently. (We have seen everything from people who walk into the room with a couple of three-ringed binders filled with what they have observed, to those who say they have kept all the notes in their head.)

To make things easier, hand out index cards before the workshop and have everyone write down their observations beginning with one of the following three phrases: "I saw." "I heard." "I read." The consistency of format will make the process of developing insights easier. Once that is done, the observations need to be shared. Posting them on the wall is one way. An even more effective approach is to have everyone write up their observations before the meeting and send it to one person who will collate them and email all the observations to every attendee before the meeting begins. That way you can start the workshop by talking about what everyone has found and group those observations into themes. At this point, strive to create themes that are functional. For example, people should have observed that the targets were looking for simpler solutions; that they are looking for things that are more efficient, faster, and easier.

Once you have the observations, you can develop insight statements written in the format of the equation we discussed earlier and then sort them into themes (see Figure 3.3). The best themes tend to be more emotionally driven: People are looking for products they could use with confidence, for example, or products that will give them a sense of belonging or fulfillment.

Things may look promising at this point, but just to be sure, subject what you have found to the decision tree in

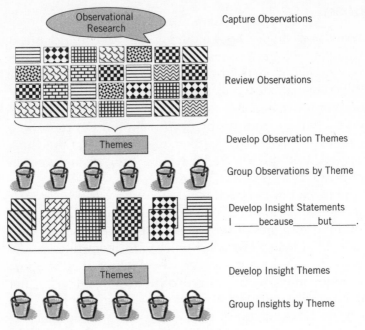

Figure 3.3   Observations and Insights into Themes

Figure 3.4. If you make it to the bottom of the decision tree, congratulations, you have a potential insight.

All in all, you will probably come out of this exercise having somewhere in the neighborhood of 25 to 50 insights. At that time, you can then again group "like" things together by the themes you have identified (see Figure 3.5).

The goal is to come out of this with about four huge themes (or what we call *insight platforms*). You can then take these insight platforms into an ideation session where you generate new product ideas against the needs you have discovered.

Putting the Process to Work in an Example   Let's see how this process plays out in practice using a fictional example: Acme Co., maker of high-end vacuum cleaners. Since 1905, Acme has sucked up profits, but recently they have been sucking wind and revenue has taken a nose dive. The company is

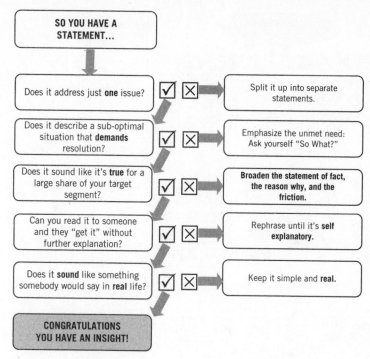

Figure 3.4   Decision Tree

looking for a new profitable segment and they think they have hit on it. Their target—and remember, you always want to have a target in mind—is high-income couples who have a strong penchant for a clean house. The folks they have in mind are borderline obsessive. They had a cleaning service, but were never really satisfied by the job that it did.

Clearly this is a defined market. But remember we want the target to be as specific as possible. Based on some very quick preliminary research, Acme narrowed down their potential target even further to:

- Adults ages 35–54,
- Who don't have kids (you can either have an immaculate house or children, you can't have both; we speak from personal experience), but

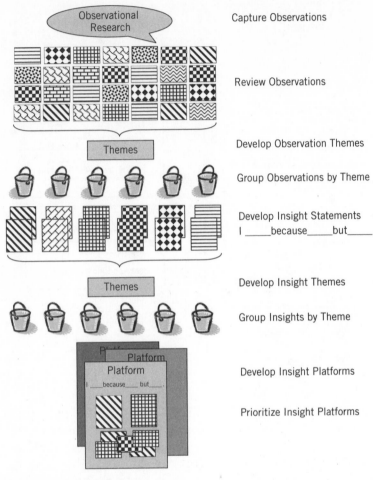

Capture Observations

Review Observations

Develop Observation Themes

Group Observations by Theme

Develop Insight Statements
I _____because_____but_____.

Develop Insight Themes

Group Insights by Theme

Develop Insight Platforms

Prioritize Insight Platforms

Figure 3.5   Workshop Process

- Who do a serious job of cleaning at least once a week, and
- Like to show off their homes and entertain frequently.

Having identified this segment, Acme goes into the field and observes the target couples cleaning and talks to them while they vacuum, taking photos and video along the way.

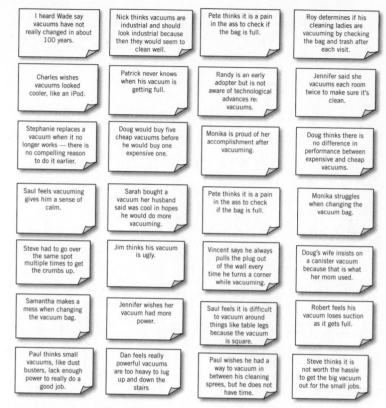

Figure 3.6   Sample Observations

Everyone is taking constant notes and by the time they come back from the field they have anywhere between 200 to 500 observations depending on the number of interviews. (If you want to put an arbitrary limit on when you can stop making observations, pick 500. Beyond that it becomes unmanageable. To simplify things you may want to go through all the observations before the workshop and identify the ones that are essentially the same and put them on the same index card.)

Upon return, a sampling of what Acme found (shown in Figure 3.6) is posted on the wall as everyone arrives.

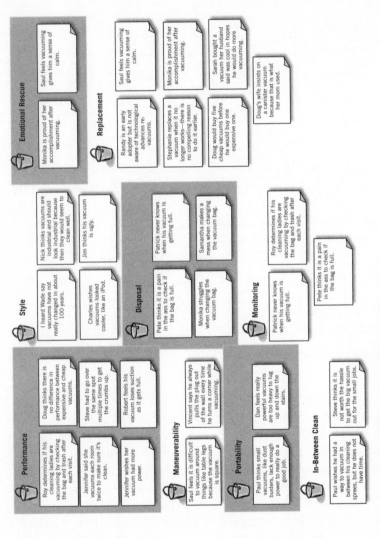

Emotional Rescue

Monika is proud of her accomplishment after vacuuming.

Saul feels vacuuming gives him a sense of calm.

Replacement

Saul feels vacuuming gives him a sense of calm.

Randy is an early adopter but is not aware of technological advances re: vacuums.

Stephanie replaces a vacuum when it no longer works—there is no compelling reason to do it earlier.

Doug would buy five cheap vacuums before he would buy one expensive one.

Monika is proud of her accomplishment after vacuuming.

Sarah bought a vacuum her husband said was cool in hopes he would do more vacuuming.

Doug's wife insists on a canister vacuum because that is what her mom used.

Style

Nick thinks vacuums are industrial and should look industrial because then they would seem to clean well.

Jim thinks his vacuum is ugly.

I heard Wade say vacuums have not really changed in about 100 years.

Charles wishes vacuums looked cooler, like an iPod.

Disposal

Patrick never knows when his vacuum is getting full.

Samantha makes a mess when changing the vacuum bag.

Pete thinks it is a pain in the ass to check if the bag is full.

Monika struggles when changing the vacuum bag.

Monitoring

Patrick never knows when his vacuum is getting full.

Roy determines if his cleaning ladies are vacuuming by checking the bag and trash after each visit.

Pete thinks it is a pain in the ass to check if the bag is full.

Performance

Roy determines if his cleaning ladies are vacuuming by checking the bag and trash after each visit.

Jennifer said she vacuums each room twice to make sure it's clean.

Jennifer wishes her vacuum had more power.

Doug thinks there is no difference in performance between expensive and cheap vacuums.

Steve had to go over the same spot multiple times to get the crumbs up.

Robert feels his vacuum loses suction as it gets full.

Maneuverability

Saul feels it is difficult to vacuum around things like table legs because the vacuum is square.

Vincent says he always pulls the plug out of the wall every time he turns a corner while vacuuming.

Portability

Paul thinks small vacuums, like dust busters, lack enough power to really do a good job.

Dan feels really powerful vacuums are too heavy to lug up and down the stairs.

In-Between Clean

Paul wishes he had a way to vacuum in between his cleaning sprees, but he does not have time.

Steve thinks it is not worth the hassle to get the big vacuum out for the small jobs.

Figure 3.7   Acme's Observations Sorted into Themes

48

Now, per Figure 3.3, we need to identify themes for the observations. Usually, you end up with 10 to 15 themes. In the case of Acme, they could look like those (performance, style, maneuverability, etc.) in Figure 3.7.

As you can see, some of the observations could have fit under a number of themes. Deciding where to put them is part of the art of the innovation process. There is no hard and fast rule.

Now, with the observations sorted, it is time to turn them into insights. Using the observations, small teams create insight statements by turning the observations into the equation [I (insert "fact" here) because (insert "why" here) but (insert "tension" here)].

Figure 3.8 shows how that might look for two of the themes Acme uncovered (performance and in-between clean).

Performance Insights

Once I get cleaning I don't want to stop because I want to get on to more enjoyable things, but I lose pace when I realize that the vacuum was not actually sucking up anything.

I vacuum often because it gives me sense of accomplishment, but that feeling is dashed when I realize that the vacuum was not actually sucking up anything.

My vacuum cleans the large areas well because it is powerful, but I wish it was a bit easier to maneuver in tight areas.

I keep a clean house because it keeps me/my family healthier, but I never know if my carpets are really clean.

I am willing to pay more for certain things because I know I will get better performance, but when it comes to vacuums there is no real difference between brands.

In-Between Clean Insights

I clean the house once a week because that is what I have time for, but I wish there was a way to easily do the "in-between cleans".

I do "in-between cleans" often because keeping a clean house calms me, but getting all the stuff out for a small job ends up being more stressful than it's worth.

My main vacuum for the house is pretty good because it has a lot of suction, but it is a pain in the ass to get out for smaller jobs.

Figure 3.8   Breakout of Two Insights

Generally you will end up with about 50 insight statements at this point in the workshop. All the insights are hung on the wall. Participants review them and themes are developed. Usually you will end up with about 10 themes. Here are some of the themes that emerged from the insights for Acme Vacuum: pride, accomplishment, confidence, no sacrifices, pain reliever, and get smart. And you can see how the insights fit under the themes in Figure 3.9

The last step of this process is to take each bucket of insights and "ladder up" to find a final set of insights for testing.

Laddering

The idea of laddering has been around for more than 40 years and it is a concept we love. Laddering is a great way to find the emotional resonance in your insight. And it isn't very complicated. All you need to do is ask "why" over and over again.

An example will show you what we mean. If you were talking to people about their health, you might hear: "I really need to exercise because I have to lose some weight, but I can't seem to find the time to go to the gym."

That sounds like a solid insight. It certainly is in the proper equation format we suggested in previous examples. But it doesn't seem to have an emotional component. We say "seem" because if you dig a little deeper, you might find that missing emotional piece. How do you do that? By consistently asking "why" in your conversations with your target.

Let's say you make exercise equipment and your target did, indeed, say they wanted to drop a few pounds. You would ask them why and you might hear:

"Well, I wouldn't mind having more energy."

Why?

"I want to be active so I can live longer."

Insights

Pride

- I vacuum often because I like things to look sharp, but the vacuum itself is a real eyesore.
- I spend a lot of time shopping for the coolest stuff because everything I own is a reflection of my style, but when it comes to cleaning products/equipment there is a glut of options out there.
- We have spent a lot of time getting the house looking the way we want it because it's a reflection of our personality, but we are struggling when it comes to the contents in the laundry room/utility closet.

Accomplishment

- I vacuum often because it gives me sense of accomplishment, but that feeling is dashed when I realize that the vacuum was not actually sucking up anything.

Confidence

- I keep a clean house because it keeps me/my family healthier, but I never know if my carpets are really clean.

No Sacrifices

- I am willing to pay more for certain things because I know I will get better performance, but when it comes to vacuums there is no real difference between brands.
- I won't sacrifice power for portability because getting things clean is the #1 priority, but my vacuum is a pain in the ass to lug around the house.

Pain Reliever

- Once I get cleaning I don't want to stop because I want to get on to more enjoyable things, but I lose pace when I realize that the vacuum was not actually sucking up anything.
- My vacuum cleans the large areas well because it is powerful, but I wish it was a bit easier to maneuver in tight areas.
- My main vacuum for the house is pretty good because it has a lot of suction, but it is a pain to get out for smaller jobs.
- My vacuum is great for cleaning the main floor of the house because it is powerful, but it just about kills me when it comes to stairs.
- I clean the house once a week because that is what I have time for, but I wish there was a way to easily do the "in-between cleans".
- I do "in-between cleans" often because keeping a clean house calms me, but getting all the stuff out for a small job ends up being more stressful than it's worth.
- My main vacuum for the house is pretty good because it has a lot of suction, but it is a pain in the ass to get out for smaller jobs.

Get Smart

- I like to think I keep a clean house because I put a lot of energy toward keeping it that way, but I wish there were a way to know when it really needs cleaning.
- I vacuum a lot because I want to make sure the house is as clean as it can be, but I never know when the vacuum is getting full.

Figure 3.9   Insights Broken Out into Themes

51

Why is that important?

"That's easy: I have two young children and I want to see them grow up, strive for their dreams, and live full lives. They're my reason for being."

Notice what happened in a simple conversation. We went from "wanting to shed a few pounds" to "my children are my reason for being." Just a few simple "whys" got us to a much richer and higher emotional order, and the need became extremely compelling. We're willing to bet this new insight statement leads to a much richer outcome than the first.

Now, the concept is called laddering for a reason. Consider what would happen if you sold office equipment. The insight statement might be:

"I need an office chair with four legs, but they're just not comfortable."

Why is it important that your chair has four legs?

"Because it stops me from falling over."

Why is that important?

"So I don't hurt myself."

Why is it important that you not hurt yourself?

"So that I can keep working."

Why is that important?

"So I can provide for my family."

Why is that important?

"Because they are the most important thing in the world."

In your marketing, you wouldn't suggest someone buy a new office chair to show her family she loves them. You might move down a rung and concentrate on the fact that a better chair allows someone to be more productive. But you get the point. Once you have an insight be sure to subject it to laddering to make sure it is as strong and compelling as it can be.

Let's see how it plays out in Acme's case using the first insight under "pride" in Figure 3.7.

> *You told us that you vacuum to make things look "sharp." Why is that important?*
>
> "I want to have everything neat and immaculate."
>
> *Why is that important when it comes to your carpets?*
>
> "Because clean carpets look nice."
>
> *Why is that important?*
>
> "Because others will notice.
>
> *Why is that important?*
>
> So that everyone can see that I keep a good house."
>
> *Why is that important?*
>
> "So I look good to my friends."
>
> *Why is that important?*
>
> "Because their opinion is a reflection of who I am."

Going through this exercise led Acme, Co., in the prior example, to express their insight platform this way:

ProClean: "I have a real sense of pride when it comes to cleaning because it's a reflection of who I am and my attention to detail, but vacuums don't meet my demands."

Speaking of Emotion The previous process depicts a hard, rules-driven, left-brain discussion about how to find the best insights. But we also want to give you four "squishy" right-brain thoughts you can use to make sure the left-brain insights you came up with are correct.

1. Is there energy around the room? When you come up with a terrific insight, it resonates with people in the workshop—and outside of it.
2. Does it feel like a big problem that needs to be fixed? Yes, of course, you are going to test for this (as we will talk about in Chapter 7). But when you have hit on a big idea, you know. Do you feel that way here?
3. It generates oodles of ideas. How do you know when an insight is potentially significant? Here's a simple test. If you say your thought out loud and in a matter of minutes can dream up dozens (if not more) ideas, you are onto something.
4. Are you creating evangelists? If the need is big enough, and your solution is wonderful enough, customers/ consumers will talk about what you have to all their friends. This is true whether we are discussing computers—Apple—or hamburgers—Five Guys and In-and-Out.

"It's a wonderful need . . . just not for us."

There is one more HUGE check you need to undertake before setting off to develop the insight into something you can sell. You must make sure it is a good match for your organization. You would be amazed by a) how often people omit this step and, b) how many times you can come up with a truly wonderful insight and still decide (correctly) that going ahead is NOT a good idea.

Let's take the potential problems individually:

1. **The need you are solving for must be consistent with your brand in the potential customer's eyes.** Smuckers, known for its jams and jellies, thought it had a logical add on: pickles. The product seemed to be an ideal fit on the surface. The company knew how to make food that would stay fresh on the supermarket shelf and it already had the necessary distribution in place. (It could put the pickles on the same trucks that

transported its existing products to supermarkets.) So, with much fanfare, the company launched Smuckers pickles and . . . the product failed. People just would not accept a sour tasting product from Smuckers.

2. **Your channel can't sell it.** We once worked for an oil additive company, a firm that helps your car engine run better and use less gas. In the course of looking for insights, we found a huge one. Most of their customers were do-it-yourselfers who got all kinds of outdoor dirt on their tools as they worked on their cars. There was a screaming need for an outdoor cleaner you could use that did not contain water—which would damage the machinery they were working with and on. Since the company was a chemical company, the firm had the capabilities to create the cleaner. They did—and found their folks could not sell it. First, their relationships were with engine additives buyers, not buyers who purchase cleaners. And second, many of their customers—the auto parts stores— just didn't have a "cleaning" aisle in their shops.

3. **It's actually too disruptive.** We have helped clients that have products and services that would literally redefine how entire industries would do business. But instead of being a good thing, it simply proved too radical. Companies—especially large companies—can have literally billions of dollars invested in infrastructure and it would be virtually impossible to convince them to scrap that unilaterally, even in exchange for a potentially huge payoff.

4. **It is against your core values**. You are a promotions company. You can help market anything and you have come up with a wonderful way to promote casinos. There is only one problem. Your company believes gambling is wrong.

5. **Somebody can do it better.** In the course of trying to figure out a better way of handling invoices, you realize this is a huge need for everyone. The problem?

You have no software development expertise. You could gain/buy it, of course, but it would distract you from your core business.

If you face one of these five situations, do you ignore the great need you have discovered? You don't have to. You could start another company/division to handle it, or license it, or sell it. For example, Redbox, the movie rental company, started within McDonald's when the hamburger chain was searching for a way to drive more people to their stores. It tested well and wound up being a great business but it didn't exactly fit what McDonald's was all about. McDonald's venture arm decided to cash in on it by selling it.

The lesson here is: just because the idea isn't right for you, it doesn't mean it can't somehow be profitable for your business.

When Searching for Needs, Keep These Things in Mind

There are a few key things you should keep in mind when you begin your journey in searching for market needs. They include bringing in the company's sales force, adding diversity into your insights, and reinventing existing ideas into new applications. Let's take these ideas one at a time.

Teambuild: Harness the Power of the Sales Force

We've done lots of work with companies that are sales-driven. Our first customer (nearly 20 years ago) was Superior Coffee & Foods—now part of Sara Lee. We've also helped Keebler create new products for Sam's Club and Costco, and worked with food-service and manufacturing giants driven by sales forces that have an insatiable desire for new products. In addition, we've done a lot of work lately with agent-driven industries like life insurance.

We know salespeople. And we know you, the companies in the marketplace. You are looking for the big home run innovation to put your business over the top. That's great. You should. But salespeople are all about focusing on the here and now. They need something new to sell tomorrow. That's good for you and good for them. The excellent news is the innovation bar can be set fairly low when it comes to satisfying what the sales force needs.

Salespeople are often happy with evolution, not revolution. For example, take variations like those in this fictional example of a product called SparkleFingers:

- SparkleFingers Wipes with new conditioner
- SparkleFingers Wipes with a new, resealable top
- SparkleFingers Wipes in a portable container
- SparkleFingers Wipes "now with static guard"
- SparkleFingers Wipes with Rain Forest scent
- SparkleFingers Wipes with color enhancer

These types of ideas, often created in response to a competitor's product, are usually easy to come up with and to execute. If the sales group likes these ideas, they tend to be successful because the salespeople work harder to make them a reality. (It also becomes easier to fill the evolutionary side of what we call your innovation portfolio, which we'll talk about in Chapter 6.)

Sales Teams as Innovators   Salespeople are great innovation advocates. They get excited. They know a ton about your customers and their business. They'll fight for their own ideas and turn them into a success. If you can harness what your sales team knows and the energy they bring, you will have a huge competitive advantage. In fact, if you are trying to create a culture of innovation in your company, starting with the sales group is often a great first step.

But how do you bring them on-board? Here are three ideas:

- Turn them into anthropologists. Arm them with video cameras or explorer journals. Ask them to capture competitive insights, opportunities, or what's on their wish lists. They see things out there that you should know about. They may also turn the cameras on your customers. There's nothing like a customer saying they want something on camera to get things moving.

- Enlist the alpha influencers. Sales teams are like packs. There is an alpha. Actively tapping these influencers is amazingly powerful. Imagine having them present your (their) innovation pipeline. We recently used this technique and got a standing ovation from 200 insurance agents for presenting an idea that one of them had come up with (that we modified and tweaked.) Remember: People support what they create. Make it a point to create with the people who have the loudest voice in your organization.

- Educate. Periodically, stop and inform the sales group about the techniques you are employing in your search for the huge market need. Make sure they are a part of the story. Share research findings with them. Make them appreciate the rigor that their great ideas and thoughts deserve. Think of as many ways as you can to tell them that the work you are doing together is critical. That will help them contribute to both potential short-term and long-term wins.

Another way to create those wins: Get more people involved.

Diversity: Don't Innovate Without Incorporating It

To make an important point, let's start with a joke: A white guy, a white guy, and a white guy walk into a bar . . . did we lose you yet? Thought so. Nothing interesting was going to come from that joke. Why? Because humor only works when you have an unexpected and compelling outcome. The same is true about innovation. And one way to create unexpected, compelling outcomes is by adding diversity into your innovation process—getting ideas from people of different ages, genders, races, and ethnic backgrounds; getting people with varying perspectives, personalities, experiences, mindsets, and so on, involved as you go about searching for a huge market need.

When most think about the topic of diversity, however, it is invariably in terms of "inclusion," "multicultural acceptance," and "global integration."

All of these terms have tremendous merit, but they are a trap. One minute, you are in charge of an innovation initiative and the next minute, you are thinking like someone who has Equal Employment Opportunity responsibilities? This is not your job. Yes, your company needs to think this way but you are responsible for hardcore growth results from marketing and new product development.

If you start thinking about diversity in terms of growth, profit, and innovation, you will elevate the value of diversity far beyond the words in the employee handbook. In fact, you are bound to come up with a formula that looks like this:

$$\text{Diversity} = \text{A lot of new eyes looking in different ways to discover market needs.}$$

This formula can be broken down into three parts:

1. **Understanding.** If your workforce mirrors the diverse demographics and cultural aspects of your customers, you are bound to have a better understanding of your audience, providing that those diverse people have a voice in the ultimate decision making. If you keep letting the same old people at the top continue to make decisions in the same old ways, you will not have gained a thing.

2. **Credibility.** If your workforce looks like the people you are trying to reach, you increase the odds of closing the sale. People like to buy from people who look, sound, and act just like them. It's human nature.

3. **Connectedness.** If your workforce is the same as the people you are trying to reach, you are bound to have

a better handle on what is going on in the marketplace. That can give you a leg up on the competition.

The takeaway from employing diversity strategies is clear: Diversity makes a company more capable—because you are adding more skills—and smarter because you are drawing on more, and different, brains.

> Innovation success is driven by the ability to make connections.

Innovation success is driven by the ability to make connections. After all, that is what discovering an insight is all about by definition. That's where the benefit of diversity comes in. It provides a different lens and allows us to see the world in a different way. This is why the open innovation movement has been so productive. The more (different) inputs we have to work with, the better chance we have to make connections.

And that is true whether we are talking about what is going on inside our companies or in the marketplace in general. That brings us to what we want to talk about next.

Steal: Reinvent Existing Products with an Eye toward Innovation

We know stealing is an innovation strategy that could be considered counterintuitive. But that's one of the reasons we are so smitten with it. The point here is simple. Innovation doesn't have to mean entirely new. For example, vending machines aren't new. But have them dispense movies and you get the aforementioned Redbox, the video rental company. And data storage has been around for as long as there has been data. But combine it with the record store and you get iTunes.

One of the most effective things you can do is reinvent someone else's idea. There are countless variations on this theme. For example, if you are a small company, riding on the coattails of your far-larger competitors can be wonderfully effective. You can bet that Starbucks spent a lot of time and money before it came up with the idea of attaching a "sleeve" to its coffee cups to make it possible for consumers to hold a hot cup of coffee without scalding their hands. Today, you would be hard-pressed to find anyone selling coffee to go who doesn't automatically do it as well.

Rather than instructing our clients and teams to steal (which just sounds nasty), we coach them to "parallel engineer." That's our term for examining how other industries, who are offering the same benefits you do, are positioning their products and services.

Here's a simple example. You are in the pet food industry and one of the things impossible to miss is that people tend to treat their dogs and cats like children; furry children to be sure, but children nonetheless. How do the makers of children's products sell food? Many times they do it on the basis of a reward ("you deserve a break today") or nutrition. And so, you can sell your pet food the same way. For instance: "Builds strong bodies 12 ways." The bodies in this case just happen to belong to dogs and cats.

> Parallel engineering is examining how your competitors are positioning their products and services—and borrow appropriately.

If you think that is too simplistic, try this. Go to Google.com and type in the key attributes about the products and services your company offers. For example, let's say you are a marketing organization. You might say your firm creates "informed solutions," "education," or provides "qualified options," or offers "quick research" and "thought leadership."

Type all these words in quotes into Google and what comes back? Well, it turns out the following firms describe themselves the same way: Angie's List, Amazon.com, Blue

Cross, Edmunds.com, The Human Capital Institute, Orbitz/ Expedia, the *Washington Post*, and WebMd.

This is not a fluke. Type in that you are in the cleaning, protecting, preserving, invigorating, or enhancing business, and you will find firms in art preservation, car washing, dental hygiene, furniture care, lawn care, and spa treatments describe themselves the same way.

How are those firms solving problems for their customers? What can you steal? You want to deconstruct the benefits they are providing to their customers so that you can provide them to yours, too.

You Must Remember This

1. **The place to begin the innovation process** is with a need that you can fill, one that people will find appropriate for your brand. If you are known for making over-the-counter cold medicines, people are not going to accept that you also make cakes.
2. **Is it big enough?** If there are not enough potential customers for the potential need you have discovered, then the insight is not going to help you much. Remember our definition of an insight is a penetrating customer truth rich enough to generate significant ideas that can *help build your business.*
3. **You want customers to get excited.** You know you have found a big enough need when people can't wait to tell everyone they know what they found. This is how Google, eBay.com, Maker's Mark bourbon, and countless others first became hits.
4. **If you're really clear on the need that you're solving for . . .** it becomes harder to get distracted.

Coming Up Next

Once you have identified the need in the marketplace, you must come up with a product, service, or new business model to satisfy it. How you generate those (big) ideas is where we will turn our attention to next.

4

Circle #2: Formulating the Idea

Warning: This chapter may be a bit tough for the left-brained, process-driven people. We completely understand. Hang in there. If you do, you will be amply rewarded.

Circle #2 is the easiest of the three circles to implement. But that doesn't mean you want to give it short shrift. We opened Chapter 3 by saying ideas are easy (and that the need should be determined first) and we stand by that statement. We don't care what you do for a living, we bet you could come up with 10 ideas for a new product or service within the hour, if you really had to. Remember, though, we aren't just trying to generate random concepts. We're trying to deliver ideas against the need(s)/insights we discover.

As we discussed in the last chapter, in order to be successful you must be creating something that a clearly defined, emotionally charged part of the market wants and, indeed, has been clamoring for. Without a specific target to aim for, your odds of success are only slightly better than winning the lottery.

Creativity increases when you have a boundary. Just ask an artist. In his later period, when he was confined to bed, Matisse could not hold a brush. He said that the constraint of not being able to paint led to even greater creativity, which can be seen in one of his most famous works, "Icarus," created from a model made of cut-and-paste color papers which were then printed using a technique similar to stenciling.

> Creativity increases when you have a boundary.

One of the other criteria we discussed in pinpointing a need was being able to measure the ideas that are generated against objective criteria in order to make smart decisions about which ones to go forward with and fund. Otherwise whoever has the biggest title in the room will automatically have her idea carry the day or, worse, there will be complete paralysis—meaning lots of ideas but no way of deciding which one is best. This is the result of a broken innovation process.

We've all heard the stories of the CEO's spouse who mysteriously was able to come up with the "best" idea. Is this such a surprise? Absent any real measurement, wouldn't you go with the idea from the person you had to sleep with every night? In any case, if your team or client is picking ideas based on a gut feeling, your innovation process is broken.

Let's talk about a process that has been proven to work.

Beginning the Process of Ideation

You can begin the process of ideation by solving for the tension. The best way to do it is to use the words "and," "will," "does," and, "is."

- Does this idea solve the tension *and* is it . . .
- Does this idea solve the tension and *will* it . . .
- Does this idea solve the tension and *does* it also . . .
- Does this idea solve the tension and *is* it . . .

For example:

- Does this idea solve the tension *and* will it play globally?
- Does this idea solve the tension and *will* it increase revenue by X%?
- Does it solve the tension and *does* it fit within our brand?
- Does it solve the tension and *is* it feasible within X years?

Rank the criteria that comes after the "and"—from most important to least—and choose the top five to 10 to evaluate the ideas against. Later in this chapter, we will show exactly how the process works.

Make sure you talk to any person in the company who could fund or kill your project. Longer criteria lists are a sign that you have talked to key decision makers—and that is a very good thing. Eventually, you will be bringing your ideas back to these people and they are going to be checking to see if you heard them. If you have, your ideas become their ideas and you always want the support of the boss.

Get the Right People in the Room

Who are the people who are going to be solving for the tension in the way just described? Well, just as developing insights is a team sport so, too, is developing ideas. You need to get a mix of cross-functional team members, key stakeholders, "out of the jar" thinkers (see Chapter 7) *and target consumers* in the room for the highest rate of return and the biggest, best, most business building ideas. No one person can do it alone, despite what people who hold themselves out as "Creative Gurus" might tell you. So, the more perspectives you have, the better. And while some people don't like having potential customers in the room, we think it is dangerous to exclude them. After all, they are the ones who ultimately have to say "yes" to what you are creating.

So, invite potential customers along with someone from marketing, R&D, finance, legal, and so on.

When choosing the cross-functional team members make sure you also have key stakeholders in the room as well— distributors; salespeople; retailers. They not only will bring a new way of looking at the problem, but because they will be helping develop the ideas, they will have skin in the game/ ownership which will make the sell-through process throughout the organization all the easier. The more internal evangelists you have the better.

In addition, make sure that everyone in the room works and plays well with others. Don't invite "Debbie Downer," someone who likes to drop what we call "Bummer Bombs." We all know someone who in our organization has these traits. Keep them out of the ideation session. One way to include them, while keeping them out of the room, is to ask them to send someone that they are mentoring.

Finally, we recommend you have two or three idea catalysts in the room. We like to call these people "idea monkeys" because they are bold, fearless, fun, and prolific with ideas. They set a playful tone that puts people at ease and help bring out the best ideas of others by generously connecting thoughts together.

Choose the Facilitator

Can you run the ideation yourself? Of course. But we find it works better if you have someone from outside in charge. Just like a quarterback on a football team, or a conductor of an orchestra, the facilitator calls the shots and controls the action. In order to be successful in this role, the facilitator must be someone respected and a person that participants are not trying to please. That's one reason you may want to bring in someone from the outside. Just as kids may not heed their parents at home but will listen to a teacher at school, the same holds true for adults not listening to a co-worker but paying attention to someone who doesn't have an office down the hall. Additionally, if you are paying an outsider person/company, people are not as likely to show up late, leave early, or act out during a session.

We once ran an ideation session for a retailer lead by an infamous CEO. We were warned by everyone on her team that she was incredibly eccentric and hard to manage but she insisted on being part of every "big" idea in the organization so she wanted to be in the session. Having her there was a disaster. She refused to take direction and she refused to play nice. We got the team to deliver ideas by breaking up into smaller teams and literally segregating the CEO. In hindsight, it would have been better not to have her in the room. Moral? You must choose the participants of an ideation carefully—regardless of title.

> Choose the participants of an ideation session carefully, and regardless of title. Invite cross-functional team members and make sure you also have key stakeholders in the room.

Set the Ground Rules

With the right people in place, and a facilitator at the ready, it is time to begin. The following are "rules" that will make the ideation/brainstorming session go more smoothly and produce better results. Upon initial review they might seem easy but they are a bit tricky to apply once everyone's creative juices are bubbling. It is the facilitator's job to ensure the rules are followed. Ready? Here goes.

Suspend Reality/Defer Judgment   It is very important not to kill ideas before they have had a chance. Ensure that ideas are not judged before the designated time for judging. Constantly reassure those left-brain thinkers in the room there will be a time for measuring the ideas against the insight and the success criteria, but stress that the time to do that is *not* while the ideas are generated.

It is very important not to kill ideas before they have had a chance. There is a time for measuring ideas against a set of criteria but the brainstorming session is not it.

Be Positive We have all seen people use criticism as power, shooting down ideas by finding fault with them and explaining why they won't work instead of trying to build on them so they will. Make a rule that when people have a concern, they must use the words "How to," "I wish" and "in what ways might we" in response to what they hear. For example, instead of someone stating, "that idea will never pass legal," they need to ask, "how might we ensure that idea makes it through legal?" The reason this is such a powerful technique is that it allows them to position their concern in a way that lets the group solve it. The group naturally ideates to make their wish come true rather than hearing, "that's a bad idea."

One way to ensure people use the, "how to," "I wish," and, "in what way we might" phrases is to make violators wear a ridiculously looking hat until someone else commits a violation. Another way is for the entire group to be armed with Nerf® balls and the violator gets pelted for an offense. It sounds silly–because it is–but it works. (We know we just lost some of you. Got it. The hat and Nerf® ball ideas feel so far from serious that you can't believe 100 million dollar ideas could come from a process that includes them. You are incorrect. We're sharing techniques that Fortune 10 companies have been using for decades. They do it to make money, not because they own Hasbro stock.)

Generate as Many Ideas as Possible Linus Pauling, who won the Nobel Prize *twice*, said that the key to having good ideas is to come up with a lot of ideas and throw out the bad ones. Quantity is king when innovating. You need to create as many ideas as possible (hundreds in a given session) and then select the best ones. To keep you going, consider this: James Dyson went through 5,127 prototypes before landing on his iconic DC10 vacuum cleaner.

Swing for the Fences Make sure you create an environment where everyone feels safe to come up with wild, crazy, off-the-wall ideas. Even the most offbeat ideas can be tamed down or will spark other more realistic thoughts, so go into the meeting thinking that nothing is out of bounds—this is a message that the facilitator should constantly be repeating as well. We tell people it is easy to make a big idea smaller but really, really difficult to make a small idea big. Start big.

Build on Others' Thoughts and Ideas When generating ideas, work in smaller teams. If you have 20 people in the room, you might want to separate into four or five groups. As you get going, keep the positive energy high. One simple way to do this is the "Yes and" rule. When building on another's idea utilize "yes and" instead of "yes but." This is one of the first rules you learn at Second City or any other improvisational comedy troupe. The last thing you want to have happen when on stage, when you and your partners are making things up as you go, is to have the scene stop in its tracks. When on stage with another player and they make a statement: "Ah, it is great to be sitting here on the beach in Maui" and you say "Yes and the drinks are spectacular" the scene can continue and build in a smooth and positive way into a story. If you were to say "Yes, but I would rather be in the hotel" the scene takes a negative, defensive, and combative tone which is not productive, positive, or funny. The same holds true when developing ideas. (This also works in all meetings and at home—but we will save those discussions for another book.)

One other thing about this rule: Giving someone credit for an idea, that is, "building on Paul's idea. . ." lets people know you were listening and creates a truly constructive and powerful ideation culture.

Springboard Off Others   One idea inevitably leads to another, and another, and another, and another, and another, and another. At least it should. Embrace this. If you hear an idea that sparks a totally new idea, run with it and don't try to cram it into the existing idea, or water yours down to the point where it fits. Remember, the key is quantity.

Important: Don't dismiss an idea because you think it has already been done. Keep listening to the builds. You hear scooter and you think skateboard, someone else thinks of the razor—a skateboard that looks sort of like a bicycle—a fact that could take you in a completely different direction. Springboarding will help you move from ideas you thought you already had to new possibilities that will differentiate your company.

Headline Ideas Then Add Details   When generating ideas, don't get caught up in the details. Capture the idea in headline form first. Generate as many as those as possible then go back and add detail later.

Warning #1: Many leaders fear ideation sessions because they think they end with headlines. If you end an ideation session and that's all you have to show for it, you have failed. A headline is the beginning of an idea, not the end so be careful to assure the group that their headlines are to capture the essence of an idea and they will be blown out into complete ideas later.

Warning #2: The *reason* people fear that ideation sessions end in headlines is because poorly trained or inexperienced consultants actually practice brainstorming this way. Working with such an "expert" will likely end up creating bad feelings, little results, cynicism, and ugly inertia. It also may cost you your job.

Capture Your Ideas   How many times have you woken up and had a great idea only to later not be able to remember it? When in a session, if you get a nugget of an idea, don't try to keep it in your head. Write it down if you have to wait to contribute. This will ensure you'll be able to recall it and will clear your mind to participate in the current conversation and come up with even more ideas.

Write Legibly   This does not sound creative, but it is very important in an ideation session. If no one can read the ideas later then the idea is pretty much dead in the water ... no matter how good. If you are asked to write your idea down—so it can be posted on the wall, for example—make sure your writing can be read. (And, yes, this applies to physicians.)

Stretch Yourself   Coming up with ideas is hard work and your brain will hurt. Push yourself to dream, to imagine, to suspend disbelief, to trust that someone will help you figure it out eventually. There is always more to an idea if you push yourself a bit harder. (If you are a process junky, exhale. Very soon, we will need to tap your ability to converge and work on details. We're not quite there yet.)

Have Fun   Fun leads to great ideas. Feeling good has been shown to improve people's creativity and ability to solve problems. In one experiment, subjects were shown a video of comedy bloopers to lighten their mood, before being presented with a practical problem involving a box of matches, a box of tacks, and a candle. They were told to attach the candle to a cork bulletin board in such a way that wax didn't drip on the floor. (The solution is to attach the matchbox to the board and use it as a base for the candle). The experimenters found that people who had viewed the comedy clips were more likely to solve the problem than those who saw a mathematics documentary intended to put them in a more neutral mood (or perhaps to sleep.) Ideation sessions are hard work but they should not feel like it. Relax, have fun, and the ideas will come.

> Fun leads to great ideas. Feeling good has been shown to improve people's creativity and ability to solve problems.

Let Your Mind Diverge

Now that we have set the ground rules, the first step in developing ideas is to diverge, that is, to let your mind wander and come up with as many new product or services concepts as possible. There are many techniques to do this. The most effective way is to utilize "lateral thinking." Come at the problem from many different directions—straight, sideways, upside down, backwards, you name it. There are literally hundreds of different lateral thinking techniques out there. Let us share a couple of our favorite ways to boost creativity. We'll use our fictional vacuum company, Acme Co., which we discussed in Chapter 3, to illustrate how lateral thinking can work and the great ideas that can result.

> Come at a problem from as many different directions as possible—straight, sideways, upside down, backwards . . . you name it.

Let's say you are the CEO or CMO or CIO (Chief Innovation Officer) of the struggling Acme Co. (see Figure 4.1), and you have said to your team, "we need to reinvent our industry and, much more specifically, ourselves because the future of our business depends on it." But you aren't exactly sure what direction to go in. So you do some research and land on a target segment—upscale dual income couples with no kids—and uncover the two key insights we talked about in the last chapter.

People who you would like to be to your customers told you:

- I vacuum often because I care about the health of my family, but I'm not confident that my carpets are as clean as they need to be.

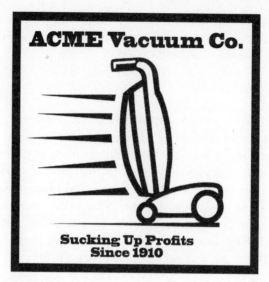

Figure 4.1   Acme Logo

- I have a real sense of pride when it comes to cleaning because it's a reflection of my professional work ethic but vacuums don't meet my demands.

You are on your way, but now you need some revolutionary ideas to deliver against these insights. This is where SCAMPER comes in, and, no, we don't mean turn around and run away with your tail between your legs because you don't have any ideas. SCAMPER is a lateral thinking exercise—whose roots can be traced back to Albert Einstein via brainstorming experts—where each letter in the word stands for something, which you then apply to solve your problem. Here's how it works.

S = Substitute

What can be swapped in or out to create something new? In 1982, Gregory Sams substituted vegetarian ingredients for meat in a burger and created the first veggie burger. Other examples include mail order. It substituted pictures on the printed page for going to the store, and later e-tailers substituted the Internet for mail order.

C = Combine

What two (or more) separate things can you put together to create something new? Home haircuts require clippers and a vacuum. The Flowbee resulted from combining the two. Food companies have put peanut butter and jelly in the same jar. There are places that combined dinner and a movie (you eat a restaurant-quality meal while watching a movie in a theater-like setting), and you can send candy along with your flowers through most of the national florist chains. And, have you ever played Frisbee golf?

A = Adapt

What can be borrowed and applied in a different way? During the recession, Hyundai adapted the concept of a warranty and created its Assurance Program. (If you lost your job, you simply could return the car you leased without your credit getting dinged.) And speaking of cars, Jeep was originally a military vehicle. One more example: Disney charges a heck of a lot for a ticket to what is basically a county fair.

M = Magnify or Minimize

What can you make really big or really small? The Hummer and the Smart Car are the simplest examples. Lowe's and Home Depot are your local hardware stores but super-sized. Five Guys and In-and-Out have reduced fast food restaurants to their essence.

P = Put to Another Use

What can you apply in new ways? In 1970, a 3M researcher was trying to invent a super strong adhesive and instead developed a super weak one. Another 3M employee used the adhesive to hold bookmarks in his hymnal. Hallelujah, the Post-It was born. The microwave oven actually was an unintended off-shoot of radar research and Viagra, and its kith and kin, were initially developed to stop hair loss.

E = Eliminate

What can you remove? The wireless phone has no cords. The touch screen eliminated physical buttons on phones. The new Dyson fan has no blades.

R = Reverse or Rearrange

What if you put things in a new order? Clarence Birdseye took the quick-freezing process that made him millions in the frozen food industry, reversed it and created the first dehydration process for food. Architects design "upside down" houses all the time (where the kitchen and living room are upstairs.) And the bustier is nothing more than wearing underwear as outerwear.

You Can Start Anywhere

Obviously, you can start with any letter in the scamper model to generate ideas—and then go through each and every one of the letters. But since we don't have an infinite amount of space, let's take one of the letters and apply this to coming up with new ideas for Acme.

We'll use **Eliminate** for this example. What can you eliminate from the vacuum?

- The wheels
- The bag
- The cord
- The attachments you rarely use
- The noise
- The spinning brush
- The manual carpet/hardwood floor switch/dial
- The handle
- The bag or canister that collects the dirt
- The pain in your back from carrying it up and down the stairs

- The dents/scrapes in the walls from carrying it up and down the stairs
- The embarrassment of how "dated" your vacuum looks (but it still works, so you don't want to get rid of it)

Now we are getting somewhere. From the above list of things we could eliminate, what kind of vacuum ideas come to mind? Remember, headline your ideas first–and then add details.

With no wheels it could be a **Backpack Vacuum**. This would also eliminate those scrapes on the wall.

With no cord it would be a **Lithium Ion Powered Vacuum**—totally battery powered. (Hmmm, maybe we could do a solar version as well.)

Getting rid of manual switches and dials could create an **Automatic Sensing Vacuum** that knows the type of floor you are on and adjusts the vacuum settings accordingly.

Only getting the attachments you really want/need could lead to a **"Design Your Own Vacuum"** store or website.

No marks on the walls could lead to a **Soft Shell** or skin around the head of the vacuum.

Keeping the vacuum from looking dated could be solved with **Updateable Shells**.

Those were six ideas from one person from one word from one lateral thinking exercise. (Told you this was the easy part.) Imagine how many ideas we could come up with going through all of SCAMPER in a room full of people that included cross-functional team members, outside experts, and consumers. More than 100 would flow out in minutes. (All delivering against the insights we had discovered. We guarantee it.)

Now let's put flesh on the bones of one of these ideas.

Filling the Idea Out

When adding detail to an idea, there are some clearly-defined areas that need to be filled in. These will help you build the idea and provide what is needed later on to develop a full-fledged concept that can be tested with consumers.

Here we give you a list of things you need to do, once you have come up with the idea. And then we will show you how it plays out in practice. Once you have the idea, you must create the following seven things:

Idea Name

At this point in an idea lifecycle the name needs to be very descriptive. This will help when reviewing concept and comparing them to one another. It will also give you a head start when it comes to creating the communication (see Chapter 5) which will link the idea to the need. To analytic people this step may seem obvious and relatively unimportant. It is not. Here you have the opportunity to create a name that captures the idea, embodies the insight and creates excitement around the idea.

We did a project for SC Johnson that resulted in, among other things, a concept we dubbed "MultiSurface Cleaner." The concept idea was directly tied to the insight that consumers wanted an effective cleaner for a multitude of surfaces but they did not have the time to switch back and forth between products. They were looking for a simpler solution. Our working name became the name of the actual product: Pledge Multisurface Cleaner.

If we had named the idea "Power Scrubbies," or something cute, the team might not have gravitated to the idea or the consumer might not have known what we were talking about when it came time to test the concept. Either way the idea may never have gone anywhere. Choose your names carefully.

Headline

Again, this needs to help describe the idea. Boil it down to the key takeaway you want the reader to remember. If you can't reduce what you have to a single sentence, you don't a clear handle on the idea. We've noted that many innovation leaders have developed the *skill* of short attention spans. They want headlines because they intuitively know that if they don't get it quickly, neither will your customers.

Description

This gets into the details of the idea; how the product, service, or business model works, the benefits, and the reasons to believe (RTB) it does what you say it will.

Functional Benefit

Here is where you outline what the benefits of the functionality are to the consumer. You explain what your product or service does well. For example, our vacuum cleaner picks up 11 kinds of dirt because it automatically senses the dirt and adjusts its settings accordingly.

Emotional Benefit

Capture the emotions you are tapping into.

Tell a Story

Put another way, you need to draw a picture of your idea. You want someone to look at the headline and read what you have to say and instantly "get it."

Tagline

A tagline brings the whole concept together and ties it up in a nice bow.

Putting This to Work

So let's put our Acme hat back on. Remember the idea of
a backpack vacuum? Here is how that can play out in more
detail, using the list we have just come up with:

> **Idea Name:** BacVac or, maybe The Deep Clean Back Vac
>
> **Headline:** The World's Most Powerful and Portable
> Vacuum
>
> **Description:** Introducing the Acme BacVac (see Figure 4.2),
> the most powerful and portable vacuum in the world.
> You wear the vacuum like a backpack. It is lightweight
> (just 7.5 lbs) and cordless (it's battery powered!) so
> it goes anywhere you need it to. With its patented com-
> pression suction technology™ (CST) it is the most
> powerful vacuum available.
>
> The BacVac was designed by an award winning scuba
> equipment designer, a team of German compression
> engineers, and a team of vacuum experts (two of
> whom worked for NASA.)
>
> The BacVac is powerful and durable enough to be used
> indoors, outdoors, and in the car/truck. And clean-
> ing is a snap with the quick release canister!
>
> **Functional Benefits:**
>> Portability
>>
>> Powerful
>>
>> Lightweight
>>
>> Easy to clean
>
> **Emotional Benefits:**
>> Confidence
>>
>> Fun. (Really. A cleaning product that is fun to use.)
>>
>> Satisfaction. (Finally, a vacuum that meets my needs!)
>
> **Tagline:** Take Your Vacuuming to a New Level

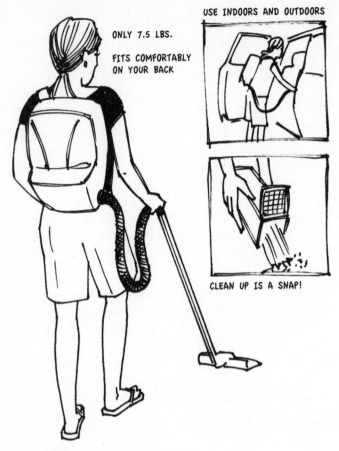

ONLY 7.5 LBS.

FITS COMFORTABLY
ON YOUR BACK

USE INDOORS AND OUTDOORS

CLEAN UP IS A SNAP!

Figure 4.2   BacVac

What Would ___ Do: Utilizing Points of Departure

That was fun, huh? Let's try another lateral thinking exercise. This one is called WW___D? The way this exercise came about has a creative story all of its own. One day Brett, a thought leader from our firm and one of the folks who helped write this book, was driving home and saw one of those What Would Jesus Do bumper stickers shaped like a fish. Being the sort of guy who is always thinking about work (Brett made us write that), he wondered to himself what would Jesus do when it come to creating new vacuum ideas. How would He approach it? What types of ideas would He have?

Realizing that some might consider that sacrilegious, Brett wondered how Steve Jobs would solve the same problem. That is essentially how this exercise works. Come up with a list of great thinkers you are familiar with and are inspiring to you. It could be anyone: Marie Curie, Ben Franklin, Thomas Edison, Cleopatra, Richard Branson, Bill Gates, Ronald Reagan, Mark Zuckerberg, Yoda, Walt Disney, Wiley Coyote, MacGyver, Miss Piggy, whoever.

Make a set of cards with a photo on each (like a set of baseball cards.)

These become what we call PODs (Points of Departure) as they will help you think differently/laterally. Once you have your deck of cards, take one and try to generate ideas for your insight just as that person/fictional character would. Think about how they manage, how they attack problems, and so on.

Let's play this out utilizing Acme Co. But just to shake things up a little, let's use a different insight. Let's say we have one that reads like this: "I think I'm pretty 'tuned in' because I have a lot of the latest and greatest stuff, but when it comes to cleaning there is not a lot out there for me."

As our POD, we will pick Steve Jobs. What do we know about him?

> Well, he is a visionary ("We will only make insanely great products.")
>
> He is innovative. (iTunes changed the music industry. The iPad may very well change print.)
>
> There are brick and mortar stores that sell Apple products as well as Apple-related products.
>
> There are a lot of Apple-related blogs out there.

Anything spark for what this means for solving our insight? Again, begin by headlining ideas.

1. There's a brick and mortar Apple Store so why not **The Acme Store**, a stand-alone outlet that sells Acme vacuums as well as "endorsed" cleaning products and even other vacuums.
2. The online Apple Store suggests **AcmeVacuum.com**, the online source for all cleaning-related things.
3. The iPod led to the idea of integrating the vacuum (maybe even the BacVac discussed before) and **adding an iPod dock** and noise reducing headphones to it.

Let's play one of these out to solve for our insight. We think the one that could do the trick is a website for Acme (see Figure 4.3). When is the last time you were on your vacuum's website? Exactly. There is some real room for Acme to own this space, don't you think? Let's see.

Figure 4.3   Acme Co. on Web

Idea Name: AcmeClean.com

Headline: The One Stop for All Your Cleaning Needs

Description: AcmeClean.com is dedicated to all things related to cleaning. It features the latest and greatest cleaning products, cleaning tips, and even "music to clean by" playlists. Site features include:

Acme and Acme-endorsed products

Indoor, outdoor, and auto: vacuums, mops, cleaning solutions

Other cleaning-related products and appliances like washers, dryers, dishwashers

Searchable cleaning tips and tricks

Special offers for members

Local cleaning service provider reviews and recommendations (like Angie's List)

Recommended cleaning music play lists

Functional Benefits:

Centralized location for all cleaning needs

Recommendations

Deals

Emotional Benefits:

Confidence you are getting the best

Satisfaction you are getting the best deal

Tagline: One Click for Clean

Again, this is one idea generated by one of the authors using one lateral thinking exercise. The power of different perspectives all in the same room is exponential both in quantity and quality.

Converge: Distilling Concepts into Categories

At the end of an ideation session you will have literally hundreds and hundreds of one-line ideas, and upward of 200 fully fleshed-out ideas depending on the complexity of what is being brainstormed. Some will be great, some good, some bad, and some really bad. There will also be some in there that are great but just not for the particular initiative/need we are trying to solve for and some ideas that are so obvious and simple that you will do them the next day.

But back to the big ideas.

As we mentioned earlier in this chapter, the key to having good ideas is to come up with a lot of ideas and then throw out the bad ones. Convergence is a key step in the process. You need to start eliminating some of the concepts you have. Too many ideas can lead to paralysis. You will have a full pipeline but never get anything in the market.

> Want to have great ideas? Come up with a lot of ideas and then throw out the bad ones.

So how do you winnow down the list? The first step is to read all the ideas and look for concepts you can group together. For example, with vacuums you might see categories that emerge such as Design/Fashion, High-Tech, Multi-Use, Retail, Customization, and so on. Then group all the similar ideas together under those categories. This makes them easier to digest.

After that, conduct some type of voting. Have everyone in the room pick their favorite three to five ideas. Secret ballot voting works best. Give each person a ballot and have them write down their favorite ideas and turn them into the facilitator. Then tally the votes and put dots on the ideas that received votes. If you start with 200 ideas you will end up with around 20. This is still too many. No company we know of is capable of launching 20 ideas in a year. You still need to converge further. Let's talk about how to do that.

Measuring Ideas against Criteria

Remember the success criteria we discussed at the beginning of the chapter? Now is the time to put it to use. Here's how.

The best way to measure ideas against success criteria is to develop an evaluation matrix. Choose three to seven criteria to rate your options against. Remember the examples mentioned earlier: Will it increase revenue by X percent, will it open us up to a new market, will it play globally, does it fit within our brand, is it feasible within X years, does it meet the insight? Make a grid and write these across the top. No matter what selection criteria you use, it should be displayed like this.

	Will it increase revenue by X%?	Will it open us up to a new market?	Will it play globally?	Does it fit our brand?	Is it feasible within Y years?	Does it meet the insight?

Once you have the top ideas tabulated, write them down the left side.

	Will it increase revenue by X%?	Will it open us up to a new market?	Will it play globally?	Does it fit our brand?	Is it feasible within Y years?	Does it meet the insight?
Idea 1						
Idea 2						
Idea 3						
Idea 4						
Idea 5						

Then create an "A" to "F" rating scale (just like in school); or great, okay, terrible; or Green (good/go), Yellow (caution), Red (stop/bad). Avoid using numbers, as you will be tempted to total them and potentially draw erroneous conclusions. The numbers will come later.

Once you have your ideas, work down each column, evaluating each option against one criteria at a time. When the matrix is complete, review it and decide which options should move forward and/or how to strengthen option(s) that scored low.

Here is what it could look like using letter grades.

	Will it increase revenue by X%?	Will it open us up to a new market?	Will it play globally?	Does it fit our brand?	Is it feasible within Y years?	Does it meet the insight?
Idea 1	A	A	F	C	C	B
Idea 2	C	C	C	A	B	A
Idea 3	B	F	A	A	C	B
Idea 4	C	F	A	B	A	A
Idea 5	D	A	A	A	B	A

Concept Development

Now that you have a handful of ideas, somewhere around five to eight at this point, they need to be developed into full-fledged concepts to test them with consumers. And while coming up with ideas is easy, concept writing is anything but. It's an art in and of itself. It's a delicate balance between creativity and discipline.

If you are having your concepts written by a person who was NOT involved in the qualitative research work, your concepts will not be accurate, evocative, or strong enough to past muster. We see this all the time:

1. Team brings in writer from the agency to create the concepts.
2. Writer reinterprets the insight and how he thinks the consumer talks about the problem.

3. The consumer hears the idea but the idea isn't the one they asked for, so it scores poorly.

4. The team hears that they have failed when the real issue is the concept was poorly executed.

The simple solution is to have your creative team involved from the first meeting until the product, service, or model is launched. Don't play insight telephone. We coach knocking down silos. This is a silo that must come down.

> Concept writing is a delicate balance between creativity and discipline.

The Ingredients: A Review

With the background out of the way, let's go over the requirements of creating a solid idea first, and then give an example of how it plays out in practice.

- **Name.** This is the first thing the consumer reads. Descriptive names work best. Try to say a lot with as few words as possible. A couple of good examples are the RAZR and ROKR cell phones from Motorola because you get what they are right away. The RAZR is thin; the ROKR also plays music. Sometimes the name is developed first and sometimes it comes last during the writing process. But no matter when it occurs, you need a strong, evocative one.
- **Insight.** See Chapter 3.
- **Headline.** This draws the consumer in and gets them to read further. This should not come out of left field or be cryptic. The headline needs to be rooted in the insight and the benefit.
- **Benefit.** This is the promise to solve the friction, the tension that you identified in the insight. There needs to be a perceivable advantage to buying this product

or service. It can be a functional and/or emotional payoff. Functional benefits are the "what it does" and emotional benefits are "how it makes me feel." Keep it single minded. Do not pile on benefits. If you talk about every conceivable benefit, when you go to test, it becomes very difficult to get a clear read on what the consumers are responding positively or negatively to. The benefits should be unique to the product and written in the second person utilizing "you" and "your."

- **Description** including a) the benefit you are offering and b) the Reason to Believe (RTB.) The RTB is the explanation of how the benefit is achieved; why it works; why it is better than what is currently out in the marketplace; and why what you are saying should be trusted. When writing these avoid internal buzzwords and overly-technical language (unless you are writing for a very technical audience.) Internal buzzwords won't mean anything to your customers and consumers are not often swayed by complicated technical words. It is important to provide rational and emotional reasons to believe.

- **Other Relevant Details.** At the end of the concept you can add more information to aid in the understanding of the concept. (Things like additional flavors, sizes, packaging options, and processes.)

- **Visuals.** Visuals are not mandatory. If used, they need to help elevate and explain the concept. Illustrations or photography are acceptable depending on which best help communicate the idea. It is important not to mix illustrations and photography in a given test— that is, you don't want someone to compare a concept with an illustration to one with a photograph—and don't have one concept be in black and white and the other in color. You don't want people making decisions based on the art.

- **Tagline.** This is the essence of the idea in one short sentence. The key is to keep it short. It is a good idea to play off and relate it to the headline.

Testing What You've Come up With

A great way of checking what you have come up with after going through the processes in this chapter is using the "80 x 30" test. Are you presenting what you have to say in 80 words or less and can you read it in 30 seconds or faster. If the concept fails either one of these "requirements," go back and double check your work. For example, make sure it is tightly focused and selling only one thing. Keep adjusting your message until you can pass the test.

> Can you communicate your concept in 80 words or less? Can you read your concept in 30 seconds or less? If the concept fails either one of these "requirements," go back and double check your work.

While you are doing this, make sure the language is consumer-centric and easy to understand. Read it silently and aloud. Double check that you are not making hyperbolic claims ("the greatest X in the history of the world") because that will trigger low believability scores, even if your product is actually truly wonderful.

Three other litmus tests:

1. **Consistency.** When testing concepts, consistency is king! You need to be consistent in structure, style, and voice. The key is to have concepts measured on the strength of the idea and avoid having one concept score better than another based how it looks or sounds. As we mentioned when we were talking about visuals, you want people comparing the proverbial apples to other proverbial apples.
2. **Stickiness.** Good concepts are easy to remember. After reading it once, your audience should be able to feed back your message in a single sentence. (If their words are better, use them.)

3. **Hearts and Heads.** A good concept speaks to both the hearts (emotional) and minds (functional) of consumers. A good test is what we call the 1 to 10 Pre-Test Test. This is a subjective evaluation you conduct before you subject your concepts to a consumer test. On a scale of 1 to 10, your concept should score at least an honest seven or higher when compared to what is already on the market when it comes to:

Relevancy
Uniqueness
Excitement
Competitive advantage
Money-making potential for your organization
Feasibility
Brand fit

If it doesn't you still have some work to do before you spend a lot of money testing the concept with consumers. Again, check the language you are using and make sure you are really solving for the insight.

Concepts Quick Reference Guide

After you've run through the various tests, perform this check on what you've come up with:

- ❐ Do you have a (terrific) product name?
- ❐ Does your brief description/headline draw the consumer in?
- ❐ Do you have a true/relevant insight?
- ❐ Is your insight addressing just one issue?
- ❐ Does your benefit provide a solution to the issue?
- ❐ Does the RTB support the benefit?
- ❐ Does the headline support the insight and benefit?
- ❐ If there are "other relevant details" do they aid in the understanding of the concept?

- ❏ Does the tagline leave the consumer with a clear, concise last thought?
- ❏ Does your concept pass the 80 × 30 test?
- ❏ Is the language consumer-centric?
- ❏ Is it logical and "sticky"
- ❏ Does it talk to consumers' hearts and heads?
- ❏ Does it pass the 1 to 10 Pre-test Test?

If all of these boxes are not checked you may be in danger of having a mediocre or even poor concept.

Bringing This to Life in an Example

Here are some examples to illustrate a good concept. To change the focus, let's pick another industry other than vacuums to show how this could work in practice. This example shows how the same concept can be written in a number of different ways. We are doing this for a reason. You need to test your idea in different iterations.

In the examples that follow (see Figures 4.4 to 4.6), we put the insight statement first (in italics)—so everyone can tell at a glance what we are trying to deliver against. Obviously, it would not be part of the final communication when we go out and try to sell the product.

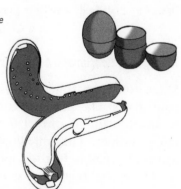

I often take my breakfast "to go" because my life is busy, but when I take fruit with me it ends up smashed at the bottom of my bag.

Introducing Fruit Armor, a full line of reusable protective fruit cases. Now you can enjoy fresh fruit whenever you want without the disappointment of having it ruined from being transported.

Fruit Armor is made of durable plastic and can withstand 5lbs of pressure. It is also dishwasher safe.

Fruit Armor – On-The-Go Fruit Protection

Figure 4.4   Fruit Armor: On-the-Go Fruit Protection

I like fresh fruit because it's cheaper than nutrition bars, but fresh fruit does not hold up well on the go.

Now there's an alternative to those overpriced breakfast and nutrition bars. Fruit Armor is a full line of reusable protective cases which keeps fruit from getting bruised before you can enjoy it.

Fruit Armor cases are only 99¢. Even adding in the cost of fruit, it is substantially less than the leading nutrition bar. And they're made by Crate so you know they're tough.

Crate Fruit Armor – A Fresh Alternative

Figure 4.5   Crate Fruit Cases: A Fresh Alternative to Nutrition Bars

I prefer natural snacks like fresh fruit because I know it's good for me, but fruit sometimes gets bruised before I can eat it.

Introducing Anvil Fruit Armor. These reusable protective cases keep your fresh fruit from getting smashed. Now you can enjoy a healthy snack anywhere.

Fruit Armor are made by Crate so you know they are tough — they are made of durable plastic and can withstand 5 lbs of pressure. Fruit Armor has been endorsed by the Healthy Snacking Advisory Panel.

Anvil Fruit Armor – Snack Healthy On-The-Go

Figure 4.6   Crate Fruit Cases: Helping You Snack Healthy

Testing with Consumers: A Bit of Foreshadowing

Once you have concepts it is important to test them with consumers. The first step is qualitative testing. Do they like it? Do they like it a lot? Do they like it more than anything else out there? This will allow you to garner feedback, which will enable you to further optimize the concepts.

Once you revise the concepts then they are ready for quantitative testing against a national or global representative sample of your target. This will allow you to determine which ideas have the most potential and you can begin to size the market potential (something we will get into in Chapter 9 when we talk about the Innovation Power Score).

An Ideation Creativity 12-Step Program

One of the easiest ways to come up with a new idea is to look at the problem differently. That's extremely hard to do if you are stuck in a rut, or you always do things the same way.

Here are 12 routine-breaking things that will give you a new perspective and open your mind to new thinking (a kind of 12-Step Program for unleashing creativity, if you will).

1. Take a new form of transportation to work.
2. Get out of your normal work environment at least four hours a week. Hold a meeting in an unusual place. If you always write reports at home, try doing it in the office (or vice versa).
3. Strike up a conversation with a complete stranger.
4. Take a "Radical Sabbatical" with your team and experience something you have never done together before and share perspectives with each other afterward. This could be an hour, a day, or a week together. (Okay, we know, the hour is more likely.)
5. Set up a monthly lunch with someone outside your department or company and get their perspective on a problem you are trying to solve.
6. Ask your family (especially your kids if you have them) to help you solve a problem.
7. Read a magazine, a book, or a blog that you would not normally read.
8. Watch television programs that you would not normally watch.
9. Listen to radio stations or music you would not normally listen to.
10. Take a walk in a park; go to a museum, a zoo, or to a movie during office hours. (Gasp!)

11. Go shopping (to an actual store, not on the internet) for something you don't need or even want. Talk to the salesperson and ask a lot of questions.
12. Eat only things you have never tried before for a week.

These 12 steps really do work. Try them. You can thank us later.

You Must Remember This

1. **Easy but not simple.** While creating potential ideas is the easiest of the three circles that comprise the innovation process, giving it short shrift would be a mistake. The better the idea the easier it will be able to stand out in the marketplace.
2. **Ideas can strike anywhere.** Keep note cards within easy reach at all times—on your desk, in your pocket, in the car, and on the night table at home.
3. **Practice, Part I.** What is clear from everything we talked about is the more you practice coming up with ideas, the better you will get at it. If you find yourself with four free minutes during the day, see if you can come up with 10 ideas for improving your commute, your next team meeting, your workspace, your vacation, and on and on.
4. **Practice, Part II.** Record every idea you have during the day. Count up the number. Tomorrow see if you can top that number by at least one.

Coming Up Next

Once you have found a market need and identified a product and/or service to fill it, you need to tell the world what you have so they can give you buckets full of money. Communication/Commercialization is what Chapter 5 is all about.

CHAPTER

5

Circle #3: Successfully Communicating (and Profiting from) What You Have Come Up With

And so, we come to the last circle. We feel ambivalent about putting it last. On the one hand, placing communication/commercialization at the end of the innovation process is a good thing. Logically, this is where it must go because its purpose is to link the huge market need (Circle #1) to the idea that is going to fill it (Circle #2). And by definition it can't possibly do that until you have the other two circles firmly in place. Communication is the piece of the puzzle that ties everything together. It explains to people that you have solved a big problem they have, and once they understand that, they will line up (at least metaphorically) to give you their money or in the case of cause-driven organizations, their emotional capital. That's no small point. Yes, the fundamental reason for linking need, idea, and communication is to make the innovation process work as well as it can. But the real purpose is to make your organization successful. To do that, communication must be the last step in the process.

On the other hand, we feel it can be a mistake to put communication last. Not because it should go earlier in the process—as we just saw it can't—but because by making it the final thing we deal with, there is a natural tendency to be tempted to rush through it. Your thinking might go, "we have done the hard part, having identified the need and a way to fill it. Now let's go to market as quickly as we can." And that can be a huge mistake.

As we have said from the beginning, innovation is a three-legged stool; if you get the insight and idea right but the communication wrong, your launch will tip over (i.e., not stand up to the competition.) A terrific product, poorly communicated—see our earlier discussion of TiVo—ends up in the same place as a so-so product with wonderful communication: struggling to find a customer. This is what can happen if you don't spend enough time on communication, either because you are speeding to market, or—and we need to be blunt about this—you don't feel comfortable dealing with communication because it doesn't play to your strengths as someone who is naturally analytical. Communication is, in part, an emotional art and that tends to make left brainers squeamish. You don't find many mathematicians playing in the marketing department.

> Communication is, in part, an emotional art and that tends to make left brainers squeamish. It just doesn't play to their strengths.

A Brilliant Idea Badly Communicated Becomes a Bad Idea

One reason communication does not get enough attention in the innovation process is because there is an outdated belief that the effects of marketing can't be measured directly. Those of us over the age of 30 grew up with the rock solid belief that there was simply no way to track directly the effectiveness of communication—especially advertising. We even reduced our belief to a pithy sound bite (stolen from a mostly forgotten department store magnate: "Half the money I spend on advertising is wasted; the trouble is, I don't know which half." John Wanamaker, the man who pioneered the concept of department stores on the east coast, especially in his hometown of Philadelphia, is the man who said that.

Wanamaker was an innovator. Three quick examples, courtesy of the program PBS did on him, will prove the point. He invented the price tag. Before it existed, most buying was done via haggling. "A devout Christian, he believed that if everyone was equal before God, then everyone should be equal before price." He also invented the white sale, to boost revenues in January, and in 1874, he printed the first-ever, copyrighted store advertisement. "When people discovered that its promises were true, business boomed. The concept of truth in advertising earned him the public's trust, which he never lost."

Wanamaker was a huge believer in advertising as a way to get the word out about what his stores were selling. When asked one day if he was spending too much on advertising, Wannamaker replied, "I know that half the money I spend on advertising is wasted. The problem is I don't know which half."

As we said, it is a wonderful quote and one that lazy executives rely on when it comes to justifying their advertising budget. The problem for those lazy executives, and the companies that employ them, is Wanamaker's comment is hopelessly out of date. (That isn't surprising. He died in 1922.) Thanks to everything from better ways to track the link between communication and sales to advanced breakthroughs in mathematics, we are now able to figure out with remarkable certainty what works and what doesn't when it comes to a given communication in a specific setting. (This is one reason we predict that you will find left-brainers being attracted to—and in many cases dominating—the communication function in coming years.) Today you can tell exactly what part of your communication budget is being wasted. There is an entire *huge* sub-set of the advertising business— it usually goes by the name of data analytics—that is devoted explicitly to figuring out the most efficient way to reach potential customers (and an important part of their work is identifying what does not work.)

Here's a simple example. T.D. Ameritrade, the online bro- kerage firm, increased the number of new account openings that came via their website 14 percent by making very small changes to the copy, design, and images on their homepage, based on an incredibly thorough examination of absolutely everything that was there. They tested every single word, color, and design element with customers to see what about their communications could be improved. For instance, it turned out that simply by altering the sign up language from "apply now" to "get started," and changing the color of the button (from orange to green) customers clicked on to get to the sign up page made a significant difference in the number of people who became Ameritrade customers.

Want less exotic proof? You need not look any further than infomercials. Whether we are talking about someone trying to sell you an adjustable bed, Ginsu knives, or a bet- ter way to wash your car, you can bet that the marketers have tested every single word and method of communication.

If you are seeing one person present the offer, instead of two, you know a lone presenter produced higher sales. Is it a woman trying to selling you that better way to store your clothes? If so, you can bet she scored more highly than her male counterpart. And every word in the infomercial has been evaluated as well. That's why you will hear the phrase "if you order now," as opposed to "if you buy now," and why—invariably—after they have made what sounds like a good offer you will hear, "but, wait, there's more. . ." and then they will do something like double the amount of merchandise you will receive for the same price ("just pay separate shipping and handling") or throw in something else, "if you order within the next 15 minutes."

Typically what these marketers do is test the commercial—and all the variables—in a number of small markets charting carefully what a change in wording or presentation does to sales. Once they hit on the combination that generates the most income (for example: one presenter; as many shots of the product in action as possible; and a doubling of the offer at the end), then, and only then, do they take the infomercial national. If they can't make the ads work, they kill the project altogether and consider it money well spent—and saved.

Once upon a time, half of the money that was spent on advertising was probably wasted. As these examples show, that is no longer true. In fact, we will go further; advertising is becoming the price you pay for a bad idea.

In the future, if you have to advertise a product or service extensively, it will mean that there is something terribly wrong with your product. Today, social media is allowing people to spread the word more and more efficiently. Excessive advertising will be the price you pay for not having a big enough market need, or a wonderful idea, or terrific communication linking the two. If you get all three circles right—and, as we have just seen, communication is a vital part of that—advertising budgets should naturally fall dramatically as a result.

Three and a Half Rules for Improving Your Communication Efforts

Want to understand just how important communication is? Consider this: in the next decade it's estimated that healthcare organizations will spend billions of dollars marketing new products, services, and business models to serve the aging boomers and deal with the changing face of the market. With that in mind consider this sentence:

"Our wellness program's deductible has no exclusions applied to primary, in network care, outside of pre-existing conditions."

We already made the point that advertising would become the price you pay for a bad idea. Now we will build on that point: excessive marketing dollars have always been the price paid for poor communication whether the idea was good or bad. If folks don't understand what you are trying to tell them, you are wasting your money.

What follows are 3.5 ways to pay less and profit more when it comes to our third circle (our apologies to Tylenol and other pain relievers who will likely see slumping sales when our suggestions are followed).

The First Rule: Speak English

Do you know what the terms "Universal Life," "Variable Life," or "Whole Life" mean? Just like the healthcare industry (which we singled out for the sentence "Our wellness program's deductible has no exclusions applied to primary, in network care outside of pre-existing conditions."), people who sell insurance often forget that insurance professionals are the only ones who understand the language.

It is critically important that you constantly keep this in mind (and act accordingly): You are not the true experts of the benefits your products deliver—your customers are the experts. They use everyday words when they talk about their wishes, dreams, and fears. And we guarantee you that they are not naturally using the term "whole life insurance" or "wellness" when it comes to saving money or not getting fat.

If you are not using the words your customers use to describe their needs as you go about explaining what you have to fill them, you are making your job 20 times harder than it has to be and you are spending too much money doing it. There is absolutely no reason a customer should ever have to figure out the benefit you are offering (as they are forced to do almost every single time when it comes to insurance, healthcare, pharma, legal services, and any other industry that ends their marketing with mouse type legalese). Speak English. Use the same words your customers do to describe your product or service. The voice of the customer must resound clearly in all of your communication.

Rule 1.5: Hire a Storyteller   Many companies make the mistake of thinking that if enough people chime in on the communication, they are bound to get it right. This is not the case. The result is a message that is too technical, too confusing, or too bland. Think of it this way: Just because you can read a book does not mean you can tell a great story. We recommend having a brilliant writer on your innovation team. They will be able to take the most important benefits, language, and emotions that your customer is conveying and craft an evocative story that resonates with your target. If the engineers at BMW were in charge of the communication you would be bored to tears with gear ratio, horsepower, and data too technical to understand. The storytellers in charge instead ask us if we are seeking "the ultimate driving machine." Why, yes, yes we are.

The solution: Involve your storyteller in the research, the ideation, and the communication circles. A good one will be able to inspire your boss by creating a concise case for the idea, your sales team by arming them with the right words and tools to sell, and your customers by proving to them that you completely understand their needs: You listened.

The Second Rule: Get the Benefit Right

"Life insurance"? Seriously? Somebody decided to call it "life insurance"? We have a feeling that life insurance got its name because nobody wanted to sell something (that would have been more accurately) called "death insurance." (We also get the feeling that "Wellness Programs" were the result of a bunch of good-intentioned people trying desperately to be politically correct.) But people aren't buying life (or death) insurance. They are really buying benefits such as an inheritance for their kids or a paid-off home for their surviving spouse. The point: Would you rather buy "Education for All Your Kids No Matter What Insurance" or "Whole Life Insurance"? Would you rather join a "Fat-busting Bootcamp" or a "Wellness Program"? Please pass the Cheetoes. We'll take door number 1. When companies connect the correct insight/benefit (protecting your heirs) with the product (insurance) and communicate the benefit evocatively ("Don't you want your kids to be able to go to college no matter what?") something magical happens. The product or service sells.

Ironically, the best insurance salesmen know this, even if the companies that employ them don't. For example, one of the top insurance agents in the United States recently coached an audience of thousands to stop selling "disability policies." Instead, he suggested selling an insurance policy that will provide "a paycheck for life." He understood that the people buying the policies were the primary breadwinners in the family—people who took great pride in providing for their families. The idea of being a burden—of being disabled—made them feel awful. Communicating to them correctly was simply paying them the respect that they had earned.

The Third Rule: Engage the Influencers

Now more than ever, social media sites have allowed us to find those who really care the most and get them engaged in the new idea.

We can ask for their insights about how to communicate it, and give them credit; make them evangelists and carriers of the message. Once your campaign starts, they will be attached to it and help propel it. (Done correctly, social media allows those that care the most about our cause to find *us*. We will be talking more about social media later in this chapter.) You see this all the time. A favorite current example of ours is comedian Ellen DeGeneres' whole-hearted, unpaid endorsement of the website ChaCha that has real people responding to text messaged research questions. She discovered the site. Told everyone she knew about it—through her own website—and traffic soared for the service.

This idea of tapping into the social networks of others is critically important when it comes to people who sell the product directly—like agents. It is important for other advisers, too. For insurance, this would include CPAs, lawyers, and quite possibly clergy. For healthcare, it may include doctors, nurses, and even teachers. Think: Who are the influencers, advisers, and agents in your industry? When was the last time they helped you discover a need, invent an idea, and launch it effectively with terrific communication?

It is easy to think a great idea sells itself. Not always. Learn to listen to and use the voice of the customer to artfully communicate what you have while you are formulating the product itself. Your odds of success will increase dramatically.

Use Their Words as a Springboard

Let's stop here for a second. Yes, we've been saying you want to use the customers' language in describing your big idea, the one that fills the need in the marketplace. But that doesn't mean you use their *exact* words.

If you spend just ten minutes *really* listening to the couple at the next table when you are at a restaurant, or eavesdrop on two friends when they are talking, you realize that people are not always completely articulate all the time. Expecting them to come up with *exactly* the right language for your innovation is a stretch.

The analogy for us is focus groups. Imagine it is 1954 and you have gathered a bunch of people to talk about restaurants. They could tell you they wanted something new. Something consistent. Some place that would be remarkably clean and would serve the food fast. But they never in a million years would have come up with the concept of McDonald's.

So, yes, listen to the customers' language and then. . . .

Listen for the Passion

Let us give you a story. For more than twenty years a book called *Customers for Life* has been the bible on customer service. It has been translated into 20 languages and has sold more than a million copies worldwide. Great book the marked said.

Great title people told the publisher. But that is not what it would have been called, if the authors had their way. They *knew* the right title for it was: *The $332,000 customer.* The authors were convinced it was a unique title. (True.) Intriguing. (Also true.) And captured an important truth: If you can turn a one-time buyer into a lifetime customer, you can make a lot of money, $332,000 in the case of someone who buys a car from you. (One of the co-authors was—and still is—one of the world's largest car dealers.)

While the authors thought it was a great potential title, almost no one else did and so the authors kept talking to people who had read early drafts of the book and asked what message they were taking away from what they had read. They heard excited responses like: "It's about creating lifetime customers;" "This will help me hold onto someone who buys from me forever;" "I can turn browsers into buyers;" "Imagine, I can keep a customer forever!" And so it went. The people who commented couldn't come up with the exact phrase. But it became clear through their enthusiasm what was most important to them. What kept resonating was that the entire book was about capturing and then keeping a customer forever. That's what they really cared about and that's what they wanted to hear the authors discuss in detail. Since the fundamental idea was so important to them, the authors ended up using it twice within the final title, *Customers for Life: Turning that One-Time Buyer into a Lifetime Customer.* Listening for the passion paid off in an international best-seller.

This is where the emotional artistry comes into play. There are those—the story tellers that we mentioned earlier—who are incredibly gifted in capturing in words what is being left unsaid. These people can help you find the words that completely connect the benefits you deliver with the often unspoken desires of your customer. A great way to demonstrate this is through some famous headlines:

- Apple: Think Different
- AT&T: Reach Out and Touch Someone
- Burger King: Have it Your Way
- Cialis: Will You Be Ready?
- Clairol: Does She or Doesn't She
- Crest: Look, Ma, no cavities!
- FedEx: When it absolutely, positively has to be there overnight
- Friends of Animals: Extinct is Forever
- Greyhound: Leave the driving to us
- Kentucky Fried Chicken: Finger-licken' good!
- Lay's Potato Chips: Betcha can't eat just one
- Nike: Just do it!
- Partnership for a Drug Free America: This is your brain. This is your brain on drugs.
- Pepperidge Farm Remembers
- Snapple: Made from the best stuff on earth.
- I coulda had a V-8!
- Verizon: Can you hear me now?

All these headlines have something in common: They connect a product or service with real language and a human need. Great writers know how to do this. Does your company have one (or more) great writer(s)?

Giggles Matter

Here is a secret that great innovators hold close: Laughter is an amazing marker for big ideas. If you stumble across something that people find funny, there is an idea there. Dig a bit deeper and you will find an emotion—a truth— that can be highlighted with some refreshingly honest communication. Beer ads often portray men caring more about their football game, bowl of chips, and six-pack than their girlfriends. Boy is that funny. It wouldn't be if it wasn't often true. (Sorry ladies.) Develop a radar for giggles. When people start to laugh about an idea, concept, or germ of an idea, they pay a lot of attention and probe further.

Sing on Key

The tonality of the language we use depends on the circumstances we find ourselves in. You sound one way at work, another when you are with good friends on a Saturday night. Research should reveal the tone of the language and emotion common to key situations in which your product or service is going to be used. Your job is to recreate the tonality accordingly. You wouldn't wear a tuxedo to wash your car. Why would you use formal language to describe a product or service designed for casual use?

Create a Metaphor

It is not an annuity, it is a guarantee you won't outlive your money. It's a paycheck for life. Just be careful not to push the metaphor concept too far. Yes, a second-hand car could be described as "pre-owned." But a used car is a used car is a used car and obfuscation can make potential customers cranky.

Make It Memorable

We are a tagline society. In fact, we bet you recognized nearly every (or maybe even every) tagline we included above. Marketers know that attention spans are short so what you create needs to be memorable and short. You need a hook. One example that everyone who has ever been stuck in traffic will instantly understand will make the point. There you are, trying to get home. Traffic has come to a complete stop and you are looking around and you see the sign on a side of a building that says: "If you lived here, you would be home by now." Can you think of a better way to get across the point that it's possible to have a shorter commute?

Focus on One Thing

We have talked about the importance of this throughout the book and it ties to the shorter attention spans we all have. You want to stress the one benefit that is most important about what you are selling. That's why we love the Verizon tagline "can you hear me now?" Verizon is underscoring the fact that its network allows you to make and complete more calls in more places than the competition. You can bet that a more technically focused innovation team would fall into the trap of talking about a 3g, 4g, or 18g network. Yawn.

Pay Attention When They Speak

Now if you are going to use the voice of the customer to create everything we just talked about, it means by definition you need to be there when they speak. You would be amazed at the number of times that does not happen. Far too often the people trying to create the communication are hearing what the customer said second or third or fourth hand. (Someone who was out in the field with the customer tells someone else what they heard the customer say. That person tells someone else who [finally] tells the person in charge of creating the communication what was said.) The problems with this are obvious.

First, you have what we refer to as the telephone problem. We named it after the game you probably played as a kid. In telephone, you line up a number of people and someone whispers a long message into the ear of the first person in line. She repeats it to the person behind her and so it goes until the last person has heard it. That person announces the message to the group. Invariably, by the time the final person hears it the message has been distorted so dramatically it is almost unrecognizable to the person next to them and so on—by the time the message is repeated numerous times, it is invariably distorted often dramatically. When that happened to us as kids playing telephone the results were funny. When it happens to us as adults with profit and loss responsibility, it is anything but.

Second, the less interaction you have with the customer, the more likely you are to substitute your frame of reference (and words) for theirs. Let's stick with the insurance industry by way of example. Say you are the person in charge of crafting communication messages and someone who heard from someone who had spent time with a lot of customers comes to you and explains what they think the customers have said they need.

"Do you understand?" that person who got the information third-hand asks you after relaying what they have been told.

"Absolutely," you say. "They said they need a whole life policy."

At this point, you should be wincing. That may be the product that best serves their needs. But never in 10 million years (unless they were in the insurance industry themselves) did the customer say "I need a whole life policy." If you don't understand how the customer views the problem you are trying to solve, it is going to be extremely difficult to come up with the words that resonate with them. (Author's note: If you are now rolling your eyes and thinking you know what your customer needs better than they do, put the book down because we can't help you.)

And there are other problems, as well. In the absence of direct interaction with customers you tend to impose your images on reality. You have a picture in your head of what a 42-year-old woman is. And it is certainly a correct description of someone. But it may not be the 42-year-old women who are going to use your product. And, of course, there is a tendency to superimpose what you think their concerns are for what they actually are. You'll end up substituting your judgment for theirs and that is never optimal.

To use an absurd example, the 42-year-old woman you have pictured in your head is living a *Sex and the City* lifestyle. The woman who is giving you the language you should use to sell the product lives in a semi-rural area and has two kids, three dogs, and enjoys going camping when she can find the time.

The reality is that most of the people reading this book are living a lifestyle that isn't even recognizable to your target audience. You make more money, are more educated, and well, just see the world differently. Unfortunately, that does not stop you from projecting your perceptions onto your customer.

The two takeaways from all this are:

1. You and your creative team have to be there with the mom in the mall when she is interviewed about the concerns your product could eliminate. Yes, of course, you could imagine what she is saying/feeling. But if you do, you lose the emotions behind the words, and when you create the communication, you are creating it once (or more) removed from what she is actually saying.

2. Being at the party is better than "tell me about the party." This, by the way, is why physicians want you to come into their office, instead of prescribing over the phone. They want to see for themselves what is going on, instead of relying on your account.

If you are there, you can understand what people are going through. You can connect. And the best can retell their story in a way that makes them feel understood. If you are not, you may be tempted to tell your own interpretation of events, your own story, and not the one that is going on.

This is a time you want to be inside the jar (see Chapter 7). You don't want to recast the story, bring in another perspective, or alter it any way. You want to hear exactly what the customer is saying. And then you talk to them using their own words in a way that they can easily understand. What this means is you don't want to hand off the communication. The communication people should be involved from the beginning. You want them to be involved throughout. Otherwise, you experience something like this, when it comes time to communicate about your product/service.

Remember, Your Story May Not Be Their Story

The situation was right out of a 1950s sitcom, but the twist at the end is fitting of O Henry. Friends of ours—high achievers both—got married, and because they were each making a good income they concluded one of them could stay home with their children once they arrived. They decided Bob would continue to work and Sue would stay home.

But a funny thing happened shortly after their second child, another boy, was born. Bob got cranky and resentful. Cranky, because he wasn't spending as much time with his kids as Sue was, and resentful because he thought his sacrifice—earning enough money by himself to keep the family happily afloat—wasn't being appreciated.

"I'd come home and something as simple as a pair of dirty socks lying on the family floor could set me off," Bob recalls. "I felt disrespected. Here I was completely responsible for all the bills and working 11 and 12 hour days and Sue couldn't be bothered to keep the house clean."

As husbands are wont to do, Bob didn't say anything. He just let his resentment build until one day he and Sue had a huge fight over the state of the house. And in the midst of the heated argument, Bob learned an amazing thing. Something that he had completely missed because he had only been looking at the messy house from his perspective.

"Sue told me that when it came to socks on the floor, or dishes that were sometimes left in the sink overnight, or an occasional unmade bed I should get used to it," Bob recalled. "She said, staying home with our firstborn had shown her just how quickly the time goes by. And then she added, 'so I am absolutely never going to turn down a chance to do something with the boys—be it taking them to the park or playing tag. If that means the house is going to be a mess for a while, so be it.'"

Bob had never thought about housekeeping from his wife's perspective. Once he did, he understood: a) a messy house was not a sign of disrespect; and much more importantly, b) Sue was absolutely right. Going to the children's museum or helping to restage a great dinosaur battle was much more important than having the magazines lined up at right angles on the coffee table.

Now when he comes home, and there is a pair of socks on the floor or worse, instead of getting mad Bob asks: "So what did the three of you do today?" Bob now says that a dirty sock on the floor actually reminds him of how much his bride loves his children.

Viewing the situation from Sue's perspective made all the difference for Bob. Viewing customers' situation from their perspective can make all the difference for you in crafting your communication strategy (and retelling a wonderful story).

And, next up, one more point about this to hammer it home.

"Huh?"—Clearly Saying What You Mean

This point is so basic, you would think it would be impossible for people to get it wrong, but they do all the time: if you want to communicate effectively, people need to know what you are trying to say. You'd be surprised how often they may not.

> Who the heck says "amount to be remitted?" Wouldn't "please pay" make more sense? And we know what the teachers' lobby was trying to say when they mailed a brochure that contained the following sentence to our home at election time: "State-of-the-art educational environments, with all the attendant support that entails, are a requisite precondition for both the facilitation, and enhancement of the ongoing learning process." But wouldn't it have been better just to say: "Kids need good schools."

We bet you could come up with a dozen examples of confusing language in the next five minutes, if you think about it. The sad fact is that someone outside your industry could probably come up with about two dozen without thinking much about it.

And if you have to use a term or phrase that could be confusing—because, for example, the lawyers say you have to—be sure you explain it. In English. Here's an example from Citibank (not a client) that we like. As the recent wave of consumer bankruptcies show, many credit card customers simply have no idea what the terms on their bill mean. (Sad, but true.) The following is how Citibank explains some terms that people find confusing:

> Account Balance versus Minimum Payment
>
> Your minimum payment is not the same as your account balance. If you assume the minimum is all you need to pay each month, you could owe far more in finance charges than you budgeted.
>
> An account balance is your total account debt as of the statement date. It includes any unpaid balance from last month, new purchases since the closing date of your last statement, and any cash advances you may have taken. The credit card company will also add in any other charges such as an annual fee, finance charges, and other fees.
>
> A minimum payment is the smallest amount of your balance you can pay by the due date and still meet the terms of your card agreement. The minimum is often a specific fraction of the balance, such as 1/36 or 1/48. Some people think that the minimum due is the only amount you owe, but you actually owe the full balance. You'll owe interest on any portion of the balance that you don't pay.

The point here is simple: Be very careful about the language you use. In this case, "voice of the customer" should mean just that. Customers recognize, respond to, and build from their own words more than yours. So use their language when exploring insights, writing concepts, and introducing new products. If you can't, as in the case of legal disclosure, be sure to explain the legalese in language that they will understand.

Going Commercial (or You Will Never Make any Money If You Can't Explain What You Have)

If no one knows about what you have come up with, you haven't innovated at all. If there have been zillions upon zillions of new and advanced safety products and services introduced over the past 20 years—and there have been— why has the rate of industrial accidents remained so stubbornly high? Failure to use protective gear provided at the workplace accounts for 40 percent of work accidents, according to the National Safety Council. Despite continuing workplace safety efforts, this statistic has been consistent for the last two decades.

The obvious question is, "why, given all these advances, has the accident rate not declined?" The obvious answer is people are not using the products and services provided to them.

And if you ask why again, you come to a blindingly obvious—and in this case potentially fatal conclusion: Innovative safety products work only if they are used. And if people don't understand clearly the benefits of your innovation, they are not going to use it, no matter how great it is. They simply won't change what they are doing now.

This is tragic because it is clear that the people who would be helped by the safety products don't know about the benefits associated with all of the new safety products.

It means as wonderful as the products are, the innovation has failed. Let's go back to our definition of innovation to pinpoint the problem. As we've said throughout, innovation occurs when:

1. There is a significant need or insight.
2. A product, service, or business model meets that need.
3. And there is a clear communication and commercialization strategy that connects one to two.

We'll give the safety industry the benefit of the doubt that it's addressing the right needs with the right products. What's missing is the communication that connects the two.

Unlike the insurance industry, which communicates—albeit inadequately—the benefits of its products, there are other industries that don't seem to communicate their virtues in a believable or meaningful way *at all.* Their thinking is the benefits are so intuitively clear there is no need to point them out. The problem with that is obvious, no matter what you do for a living. You simply cannot assume your innovation's benefits are apparent to everyone, let alone believable. Even with the rise of social media, it is still your responsibility to frame the benefits of your product in a way that is easily understood and passed on.

So if we go back to our original question—why aren't people in high-risk professions, such as firefighters and police officers, buying and using the new products out there—we find that there are three possible explanations. And at their core, these explanations can be reduced to a failure of communication:

1. They are not aware of the new safety regulations and standards.
2. Even if they are aware of them, they don't understand the safety regulations and standards or believe they apply to them.
3. They don't know the new products and services exist, don't believe they need them, aren't willing to pay the price for them, don't believe they'll work, don't want to change their own behavior even if it's in their best interest.

As we said, in every case, compelling communication is lacking.

When you are faced with this kind of situation, what's the best way to communicate the innovation you have developed? Understanding the emotional and psychological tendencies of your audience will shape how you go about it. You could do that by segmenting your potential audience, as we talked about in Chapter 3. If you did that in this case you would find you are facing three distinct groups:

1. Open ("Give me the information"): A small minority of people are actually receptive to change. Think of them as "the early adopters" in technology or anywhere else. They listen with an open mind to what you have to say, and then decide for themselves. They are learners and activators. What they will require is information and education, so make it readily available, accessible, understandable, and sharable.

2. Entrenched ("It'll take an intervention"): A larger group will take the attitude "I like things as they are; I'm not ever going to change." It will require an enforceable law or mandate, coupled with a penalty for noncompliance, to get them to do something different. You definitely don't show these people the carrot. You put the (large) stick in front of their face. You need to stress the risks, problems, and negative consequences they will face if they don't take advantage of what you are offering.

3. Stubborn but not self-centered ("My family and friends want me to change"; "I just had a kid. I want to make sure that I am around to see her grow up."): The majority of people you are courting will not pull the trigger until social influence or some other pressure gets them to change for whatever reason.

Your communication needs to address each group. You might be able to reach all three groups with a single message, or it could take crafting three separate messages. But how you do it is far less important than that you actually just do it—and that you use every form of media when you do.

How to Utilize Social Media: Changing the Game for the Better

Your thinking about social media should never be limited to merely marketing channels. Used correctly, social media will become your most powerful innovation tool and is very likely way more important than you think.

To date, we have invested in two companies to help us harness the power of social media. We believe in the power of online communities to help uncover insights; generate and validate new-product, service, and business-model concepts; and most importantly, create the necessary conversations that spark a new idea we can develop and introduce across the globe.

Everything it has done for us, we believe it can do for your organization as well. Our research shows that marketers intend to invest more in social media in the months and years ahead, but they have yet to allot substantial budgets for them. That isn't the way to go. And if you continue to fund social applications only as experiments, you're unlikely to be able to make an impact. You need to make a major commitment and you need to do so immediately.

> We believe in the power of online communities to help uncover insights; generate and validate new-product, service, and business-model concepts; and most importantly, create the necessary conversations that spark a new idea we can develop and introduce across the globe.

Debunking the Big Three Concerns

Our purpose here is twofold. First, we want to clarify exactly what we (and you) should be talking about when using the term "social media," and then we will address the three biggest worries about implementing it:

- The loss of control;
- The related concern that someone in your employ will make a mistake during real-time interactions with customers;
- And, perhaps the biggest misconception of all, that there is no way to measure its impact.

Simple definition first: Social media venues are a technically enhanced way—think Internet and mobile-based—of discussing ideas with people in communities. (Twitter, blogs, LinkedIn, and Facebook are the sorts of things we are talking about here.) Social media uses words, pictures, audio, and video to foster interaction. It is that interaction that makes some businesspeople nervous. We understand.

When you advertise, you have total control over the words, the images, design, and everything else. When you use social media, that ownership is fleeting. While you maintain absolute control initially, what happens afterwards depends on the audience. But instead of worrying about it, we think you should see this as an opportunity, one that you already have some (analogous) experience with.

You already deal with customers in some way—through your sales force, a call center, or even directly yourself. For the most part, those interactions work, don't they? Why should social media be any different?

And if employees make a mistake in interacting with customers via social media, you handle it the same way you currently address any other problem. You fix it and put in procedures so that it won't happen again.

If you use these worries as an excuse for not engaging in social media, you are putting yourself at a huge disadvantage. We recently addressed a national association of restaurant executives, and one, a vice-president at a huge chain, raised the "what-if-a-customer-writes-something-bad-about-us-on-a-blog-Tweet-or-somewhere-else-based-on-some-thing-we-posted" issue, as a way of defending his company's decision to not employ social media.

We listened patiently as he outlined in detail what he was worried about, and then hit him with some research we'd done about his company in preparation for the meeting. "We did a Google search about dinner meetings held at the biggest restaurant within your region," we said. "And while we found all the wonderful pictures you posted about the facility on your website, we also found troubling items that came up on meeting-related blogs—in particular, two planners went on at great length about the problems they had with dinner meetings at the place. They were specific, detailed, and said, in no uncertain terms, that their colleagues should hold their meetings at another place. There was no response from the restaurant or the chain, anywhere. The posts were three years old and yet they were still on page one of the results screen when you Googled the name of the restaurant and the word meeting. What kind of impact do you think their comments are going to have on someone looking for a place to have their next corporate event?"

The point is if the company had been monitoring mentions of its restaurants on social media, it could have responded to the complaints for the world to see. Instead the company missed its chance to redeem itself—and probably missed out on substantial revenues as a result.

Measuring Social Media Return on Investment As for the last objection to social media—that there is no way to measure the impact social media have on revenues and profits—that is just wrong. Ironically, if we probe deeper, the executives suggesting that social media's impact is not measurable don't have many metrics or return on investment (ROI) in place with most of their other marketing efforts either. You should align all your marketing with key financial outcomes/objectives and measure it in the context of those objectives.

There are numerous ways to measure social media's return on investment. A nontraditional approach has been put forth by University of California Professor Deborah L. Hoffman who argued in MIT's *Sloan Management Review* that we are going about measuring social media all wrong.[1]

She contends that effective social media measurement should start by turning the traditional ROI approach on its head. Instead of calculating the return on the company's investment in a blog (or whatever), managers should begin by considering consumer motivations to use social media and then measure the social media *investments* customers make as they engage with the marketers' brands.

What this means is that returns from social media investments will not always be measured in dollars, but also in customer behaviors (customer investments) tied to particular social media applications: How much time they spend on your site, the number of times they tweet about your brand, the mentions they give your product in their blogs. For example, the most important measure of the Maddock Douglas community is returning visitors. When we see that consistently rising—which we do—we know that we are providing worthwhile innovation content. An increase in the number of new visitors is nice but the returning visitors are the real investors. It is an intriguing way to think return on investment.

> Returning visitors is a key way to measure the ROI of social media efforts. But the returning visitors are the people who are probably going to do business with you.

But no matter how you choose to go about it, knowing you can quantify the bang you get for the buck is not the end point when it comes to social media. The real question

---

[1] *Sloan Management Review*, Fall 2010, Vol. 1, 41–49.

to ask is: "Are we getting what we want out of the conversation?" Put another way, just because you can measure something doesn't mean it matters. Sure, you can discover that 436,315 young women have commented on your blog posting about the latest in skin care, but if that activity isn't moving the sales needle, it isn't helping you. As we said, the only metrics that matter are the ones that support your objectives. Typical goals include increased brand awareness, increased sales and profits, accelerated new-product adoption, enhanced organic search ranking/visibility, customer retention, and real-time insights.

Identifying the Key Venues for Your Social Media

Now, these metrics don't exist in a vacuum. Your competition will be using social media as well, so you want to be smart about which you use. If you want something important to measure, gauge where you stand compared with the competition in context. You need to see who has the advantage based on positive/negative brand perceptions, organic search-term content/ranking, visibility, and their observable overall social strategy.

As you go about this, we have two suggestions. First, you want to identify the key social media most used by your customers and then evaluate their choices by not only popularity but also how believable your customers think they are. A case study will show you what we mean.

We were hired by an apparel company that wanted to start employing social media. Because you want to fish where the fish are, we began by finding out what social media their customers—and potential customers—used on a regular basis. By surveying a representative sampling of people, we discovered there were over a dozen places (including Facebook) they visited most often.

Now, that was far too many to target effectively. So we dug a little deeper and found that the apparel company's customers did not view all of those sites equally. Some websites were seen as places that were trying to sell them something. Some blogs were seen as entertaining but not reliable. Other places they visited were seen as purely social sites, so any sort of commercial message there would come across as jarring. Armed with this information, we were able to prioritize our efforts and align the right outlets with our strategies and tactics. The results were an increase in reach and, more importantly, quality of reach.

Nicholas Kinports, founder of AdMaven and a Maddock Douglas partner, has a wonderful way of thinking about implementing your social media strategy. "It isn't about making content go viral—though that would be a wonderful byproduct, should it happen—or creating the next great Facebook application, although that would be great, too," Kinports says. "It's about structuring, and in some cases restructuring, how a business views and interacts with its customer base. The modern consumer is savvy, aware, and fully able to make informed decisions, thanks to a wealth of information freely available on the Internet. The consumer of the near future will make purchase decisions based on information gleaned from unbiased peers and influencers. Social media is the latest tool through which these interactions occur."

> Social media is about structuring, and in some cases restructuring, how a business views and interacts with its customers.

If you think of social media as that—a social consultant—the results can be remarkable from both a bottom-line and competitive standpoint. But to be in the game, you first need the desire to be social and the strategy to do it authentically. Then you need strong team members to execute ongoing core competency and follow it through, paying particular attention to the way you communicate. As you can plainly see, there's a big difference between a brand that behaves like a dabbler and one that behaves like a master when it comes to social media. The language that you use will need to reflect that. Otherwise, we are afraid, your company will be lumped in with all the others when people think about "business," and that is not a good place to be.

Mastering Communication

We believe there are three key things you must do to master social networking:

Phase 1: Architect a Proper Presence

First, you need to identify where your target is and which communities are important to them. You want to be where your customers, and potential customers, hang out. You don't want to communicate into a vacuum.

Having identified those places, you need to understand the conventions and etiquette of those environments. Every site is different, but if you keep the following in mind, you won't go too far astray. Do figure out ways to foster, nurture, and support the community you are interacting with. Don't even think about a hard sell (see Phase 2).

Phase 2: Gain Credibility Based on Your Target's World View

The content you enter in the social media arenas must be carefully selected and composed with that environment in mind. Your message and content need to be all about them and what you can do to make their lives better. This means: "Help Them, Don't Sell Them." Be unconditionally generous. Visit Nike.com, one example of a company that does this well, to see what it has done for runners. (You will find blogs and training tips, and yes, some of them are incredibly soft-selling such as, "how to find the perfect fit.")

> Your online message and content need to be all about the customer and what you can do to make their lives better. This means: "Help Them, Don't Sell Them."

If we are adequately entertaining and educating customers, they will seize the opportunity to fully engage. They will share this content and perhaps even build on it—whether you invite them to or not—because that's what social beings do. When engagement reaches this level of co-creation, we've moved into the third phase.

Phase 3: Co-Creating Dialogue Where Your Company Reaps the Benefit of Exchange

Once we have defined and built the right presence, along with crafting the appropriate, engaging content, we can begin fostering true exchange of ideas and emotions. We can listen. We can genuinely hear the wants, needs, and fears of our customers. We can be empathetic and responsive. We can be a friend first, supplier second. Social media when managed correctly is everything traditional research wishes it could be.

We can then build promotions, campaigns, and *dialogue, based on user-generated wishes,* and empower our customers to not just be a part of our story, but to erase the line between "us" and "them."

It's important for your company to build a presence in social media. These new communities are irrevocably changing the landscape for marketers and how we communicate. Increasingly we are being charged with delivering ideas that engage and influence the people in these living, breathing, and highly responsive human communities. We need to integrate our message and presence effectively, profitably, and appropriately into social media communities.

The presence you build within social media will be analyzed, scrutinized, and perhaps criticized. However, entering this territory—which is controlled not by you but by the digital swarms of consumers and their communities—with the right voice and then nurturing that conversation in a manner authentic to your brand, your products, and your customer will ultimately have a far greater positive impact on your level of opportunity over the existing risks. However, the greatest risk is being absent from that conversation in the first place while your competition gains a powerful foothold.

> The greatest risk posed by social media in today's world is being absent from the social media conversation.

The good news is, if you are a genuinely good company, humble enough to learn and brave enough to engage, social media will provide you with exponential lift. And the better news is, if you are a socially irresponsible firm, social media will eventually put you out of business. It's an evolutionary process that allows the best companies to survive, thrive, and drive out others, and this makes us happy.

You Must Remember This

1. **If people don't understand what you have, odds are they are not going to buy it.** That's why your communication must clearly link the need you have discovered in the marketplace to the idea you have developed to fill it.
2. **The best way to communicate?** Use your customer's words, not yours.
3. **Measure, measure, measure.** Constantly track to see if your communication is being received—and understood. If you don't, you could end up wasting a lot of money.

Coming Up Next

Having covered the three key parts of the innovation process, it is time to discuss how you can put that process to work for you. We will begin by discussing how you want to construct your "innovation portfolio."

CHAPTER

6

Constructing Your Innovation "Portfolio"

Now that you know how the innovation process works, it is time to apply it. The first step? Figuring out the right mix of innovation efforts.

In this chapter, we show you exactly how you can correctly balance the four categories innovations naturally fall into, and receive the highest possible return on your investments.

Diversifying Your Innovation "Investments"

We chose that headline—diversifying your innovation investments—for a reason. Innovation and financial planning have a lot more in common than you might think.

When it comes to how you divvy up your personal investments, you have always (correctly) been told that they should be spread among asset classes (stocks, bonds, and cash) and then diversified further within the classes themselves. For example, you might hold stocks in both foreign companies and domestic ones, shares of small retailers and big high-tech companies, and every member of the S&P 500.

Stop for a second and answer this question: How much money do you have? Good. Now answer a second question: Do you know exactly where it is invested right now? Now the tough one: Have you balanced your financial portfolio recently (moving money from stocks into bonds; cash into stocks; whatever)?

Whether the answer is yes or no, the fact that you can even answer the question means that you have an idea of how much money you have and how you have it invested it. That's always a good thing.

So, here is a similar line of questioning: How many ideas do you have? Do you know where your ideas are right now, that is, do you know what categories they fall into? (Line extensions, concepts that will up-end your industry, something that could be really cool but you are just not certain anyone is going to buy it, etc.)

Sadly, when we ask these questions to even leaders who pride themselves on running innovative companies, we almost always get an embarrassed stare. They can readily talk about two or three projects currently in the works but when it comes to their entire pipeline—their entire portfolio of new ideas—they are at a loss when asked to classify what categories they fall into.

Herein lies a significant opportunity for innovation leaders of the future. You want to be diversified, and diversified effectively. The idea is to capture all the potential gains out there—the more bets you place, the greater the chances you have of being right—while minimizing risk. It's just like in personal financial planning. For example, if your investments in the small-cap growth stocks sector tanks, your bond holdings and money market funds might mitigate the loss.

You can use exactly the same "cover-all-your-bases-efficiently-and-effectively" approach when it comes to innovation. Think of your ideas, budget dollars, and people's time as assets in determining whether or not to invest in research and development, product tweaks, line extensions, or new offerings to diversify them as well.

Why? Invariably the new things you are working on present different levels of risk and reward tradeoffs. Like stocks, bonds, and cash, they are not necessarily correlated to one another—the success of one is not contingent on another. By investing in each part of your portfolio, you will be creating financial and behavioral (more on this in a minute) diversification that will pay dividends today and into the future.

The obvious conclusion: As with financial planning, the idea of hedging your bets—while making sure you are represented in every important sector—makes perfect sense.

The Four Classes of Innovation

When diversifying your innovation investments (and by this point you have figured out we think you should), the obvious question to ask is: How should you divvy up your portfolio of ideas? Before you can answer that, you need to determine which of the four classes (what we call "innovation quadrants") in which your innovation efforts fall. After we describe each of the classes, we'll outline some benefits (pros) and challenges (watch outs) that each quadrant brings.

Class #1: Evolutionary Innovation

An evolutionary innovation is technically easy with a clear customer benefit: "They are asking for it, we know how to do it, so let's give it to them."

This is the effort you extend to keep current cash cows fresh and to grow brands in the market. It's a hedge against becoming stale. It is generally the largest portion of any company's development budget, and it's sometimes overweighted in organizations that tend to "follow." Followers are companies—like the clothing retailers you find in the mall—that don't tend to create new fashion trends. They wait until something gets hot and then they introduce a variation very quickly.

Examples of evolutionary innovation would include combining DVR functions into a cable box, launching a new flavor of an existing product, or anything that you can label "new and improved." This is a place where you listen to your existing customers and give them what they want. Although the practice of creating evolutionary innovation can be relatively clear-cut, please be aware that it is a full-time job when done correctly. So if you want your team to work on every quadrant from the outset, you are likely asking too much.

> An evolutionary innovation is an innovation that is technically easy with a clear customer benefit: "They are asking for it, we know how to do it, so let's give it to them."

Pros of the Evolutionary Quadrant   The positive outcomes of focusing on the evolutionary quadrant can be summed up as:

- It creates a culture that actively listens to customers and consumers.
- Its ideas can and should come from anyone with customer contact, which can be an energizing process for all levels of the organization.
- Since your ear is always to the ground, you quickly know when something in the market is changing.
- It is fundamental to a culture of innovation and thus a great place to start.

Evolutionary Quadrant Watch Outs   Some challenges of focusing on this quadrant are:

- If it's all your team does to innovate, you will be doing all your negotiations with procurement because you will only be competing on price.
- It can be mind-numbingly boring work and you will likely lose the attention of your best thinkers.

- It is often waved at by leaders who say "See? We are innovating!" When in fact they are doing nothing that is truly differentiating. In other words, they call themselves leaders but are actually followers.

Class #2: Differentiation

Differentiation is technically difficult but a clear customer benefit: "They are asking for it; we have no idea how to deliver it, but we'd better figure it out."

This portion of your innovation budget is used to make a distinction between your products and those of your competitors. Multi-touch interfaces were studied for years, for example, but Apple took on the technical challenge to put it into a mobile phone, eliminating the need for a traditional keyboard, and the iPhone went on to be one of the most successful products of all time.

> Differentiation is an innovation that is technically difficult but has a clear customer benefit: "They are asking for it; we have no idea how to deliver it, but we'd better figure it out or someone else will."

Pros of the Differentiation Quadrant   The positive outcomes of focusing on this quadrant are:

- It creates a learning culture.
- Practicing differentiation means you can command a higher price.

Differentiation Quadrant Watch Outs   Some challenges of focusing on this quadrant are that:

- Striving for perfection before you launch an idea burns out the best thinkers.
- Over thinking and over testing an idea will usually result in an idea that everyone thinks is good. This is

also known as an idea that is no longer the least bit compelling.

- People can use research as a shield. ("I know we are nine months behind deadline, but there are still two more field studies we want to do to make sure we have every "i" dotted.) Ideas get stuck in this quadrant forever because it is safer to test than it is to launch.

Class #3: Revolutionary Innovation

Revolutionary innovation is technically difficult and there's no way of knowing ahead of time if the customer will accept it: "We don't know if we're on the right track, but if we can figure this out, we think we could change everything!"

This is the place where you search to find groundbreaking ideas for products, services, and business models. PayPal, iRobot's Roomba, the robot vacuum cleaner, and Fuji's environmentally safe batteries would be examples. This is a bet that the market will move toward your idea and your company will have a *sustainable* first-mover advantage.

> Revolutionary innovation is an innovation that is technically difficult and there's no way of knowing ahead of time if the customer will accept it: "But if we can figure this out, we think we could change everything!"

Pros of the Revolutionary Quadrant   Some positive outcomes of focusing on this quadrant are:

- The biggest thinkers in the organization find this quadrant absolutely inspiring. Work in this quadrant typically unearths insights and ideas that feed the other quadrants.
- Since you are swinging for the fences here, if you get ahold of a good idea, you will change your industry and potentially garner *huge* returns.

Revolutionary Quadrant Watch-Outs Things to watch out for in this quadrant include:

- It's a sexy place to play, but if it is all your teams are working on, chances are, you will run out of money before you find the big idea.
- This is where dreamers go to die.

Class #4: Fast-Fail Innovation

Fast-fail innovation is technically easy, but you have no way of knowing if the customer will accept it: "We have this amazingly cool gizmo and I think/hope/bet somebody, somewhere will really love it."

This is an approach where you go to market and do your testing and learning there. It is the opportunistic segment of your development activities (i.e., it's well within your wheelhouse of capabilities and core competencies, but far more experimental than usual). Here you expect to fail quickly before succeeding with an offering that is refined by your customers' feedback. It is fairly low risk—you don't spend much time or money before you send the product out into the marketplace—and has an extremely high potential reward as customers express exactly how they want you to alter your original idea. Google runs multiple tests on ads it is considering using, and then goes worldwide with the ones that work best. Often this quadrant involves partnerships where one side provides a missing ingredient like a brand, a channel, or a technology to the firm that had the idea. For example, P&G teamed with their rival Clorox to create ForceFlex® Trash bags. P&G had the plastic technology that made it possible to create a stronger and more flexible garbage bag. Clorox had the brand name–Glad. The union helped Clorox create a billion dollar brand.

> Fast-fail innovation is an innovation that is technically easy, but you have no way of knowing if the customer will accept it: You let the market do your research for you.

Pros of the Fast-Fail Quadrant   The positives of focusing on this quadrant are:

- It is a great place to exorcise R&D demons. Those guys in the lab coats have all kinds of cool innovations just looking for a market.
- You create a culture at your company that is always looking for win-win scenarios in the market.
- Entrepreneurs use this strategy effectively. So if you are looking for a more entrepreneurial culture, start here.
- This is also where co-creation innovation happens. This macro trend is driving innovation between for profits and cause-driven organizations. In other words, it can be great for the planet and great for profits.

Fast-Fail Quadrant Watch Outs   The main thing to watch out for in this quadrant is:

- This quadrant typically starts with an idea and looks for a need. This is a less efficient way of innovating. (As we have discussed throughout, it is always best to start with a need and follow with an idea.) That is where the term fast-fail comes from: You don't want to spend a whole lot of money up front. At the core of this quadrant is a company's desire to get out into the marketplace and see what happens.
- This is where R&D-minded, mad scientist types go to die.

How to Divide Up Your Innovation "Assets"

Now that you understand the four classes of innovation, where should you focus your attention? How exactly do you divide up your portfolio?

Overweight certain portions of your innovation portfolio. The evolutionary and fast-fail segments have the highest potential returns for your *internal* innovation group because they can get to "go" or "no-go" decisions much more quickly.

Well, with the caveat that no two companies are the same, we'd have to say fast-fail and evolutionary merit the most attention. In order to do this, though, you need to have faith in your team's ability to use customer and sales force feedback to fill your pipeline with these two classes of ideas. That's why in our hypothetical model (see Figure 6.1) we are devoting 75 percent of the resources to these two categories.

But there is a second reason we like dividing up your innovation portfolio between these two classes. They provide a healthy balance: One has you listening deeply to your current customers while the other opens you to the possibility that there may be partners who can provide you with new customers and new insights. Also, one quadrant focuses on things you are sure about, and the other focuses on things you are not so sure about.

But, ultimately, both quadrants offer your team the opportunity to quickly get to answers that green-light or red-light initiatives. There is little time wasted when using these two methods and the only thing more valuable than money when it comes to innovation is time (as in speed to market.)

By proposing that you focus on the fast-fail and evolutionary classes, are we diminishing the importance of the other two quadrants? No. But the other two are definitely more risky. They are more time-intensive and often have some side effects that are cancerous. For example, by far, the biggest challenge with the differentiation quadrant is over-thinking. We've seen far too many companies get stuck in a rut: They test and test and test concepts. Then, by the time they launch, the ideas are either too dumbed-down (they offend nobody) or too late (the competition is already in the market with their iteration of the product.) Frankly, many organizations have leaders who use this quadrant as an excuse *not* to launch ideas. They won't sell something until it is perfect and well, nothing is perfect. Their thinking is "if we never go to market, there is no way we can fail." The sad fact is that in these kinds of companies it is safer *not* to launch than it is to launch.

Think for a second. Have you ever been working on an idea only to have your competitor launch the idea first? The answer is likely yes and the reason is that you were likely stuck in this quadrant. It's an awful place to be.

When you see someone rolling their eyes when the word "innovation" is mentioned, it is usually because they have had experience with an organization that is stuck in the maddening cycle of test, test, and test some more, with very few ideas ever actually launching. Our simple prescription in situations like this is to reward people for launch *failures* as well as in-market *success*. Another solution is to leave this quadrant to outside consultants who are objective and compensated for taking the risks that your people cannot.

As for the revolutionary class of innovation, we'd all like to create something like the iPod, but these ideas are, by definition, game changing, so they most often come from entrepreneurial companies and people currently outside your industry who aren't constrained by your paradigms, fears, politics, and so on.

You don't want to abandon the revolutionary quadrant altogether, however. Working on revolutionary products is inspiring, energizing, and invariably creates new products inadvertently. A well-known cliché example of this is Tang, and all the other pens that write upside down that were created as a result of the space program. It may be a cliché, but the list is truly remarkable. NASA has received more than 6,300 patents. (Visit http://www.sti.nasa.gov/tto/ for the full list.)

A simple rule: Evolutionary innovation should come from *inside* your *halls*, and revolutionary innovation from *outside* your *walls*.

Given all of the preceding examples of the pros and cons of each type of innovation class, the odds are you will want to allocate your innovation assets as shown in Figure 6.1.

In more aggressive industries—that is, sectors such as consumer electronics that live and die by new products—you might want to have more assets devoted to the upper right side of this diagram (the revolutionary) and less to the upper left (differentiation). In more conservative industries, it's vice-versa. One size does not fit all, but the model above is a good starting point.

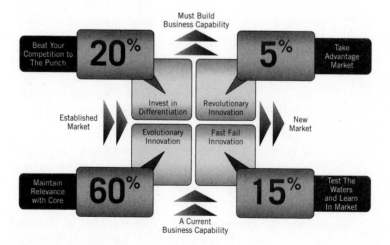

Figure 6.1   How to Apportion your Innovation Portfolio

We often hear that leaders want their organizations to behave more like entrepreneurs. If so, we recommend you focus on the Fast Fail Quadrant.

Tactics to Increase Your Success

So far, we proposed that you are probably going to spend a disproportionate amount of your innovation budget on Evolutionary and Fast-Fail ideas. Here, we offer you strategies for how you can beef up these new areas. First, evolutionary.

Techniques for Increasing Your Evolutionary Assets

Here are two simple techniques to make sure you have plenty of evolutionary ideas:

Technique #1: Employ Voice of Sales (VOS) Brainstorms: Most people in marketing have heard of "voice of customer" research, where an organization will capture customers' wants, wishes, desires, and expectations (plus the things they hate, so a company knows what to avoid) but how about the "voice of sales"?

Typically nobody has more immediate and relevant feedback than your front-line sales people. They can create the outcome you want. People support what they create, so make sure your sales team has a fun and consistent process for creating evolutionary product and service ideas.

One caveat: If members of your sales team are highly commissioned, they may hold on too tightly to products or services with higher commission rates, even when your customers are seeking alternatives.

Technique #2: Eavesdrop: It's rumored that in the early years, Michael Dell would have his call centers keep small notes on all customer feedback. He would spread these notes out on a table and read them like tea leaves, then create services and products in response to what he saw in the notes. Auditing your call center, attending research sessions, and participating in online discussion boards are all simple, proven ways to hear customer/channel/distributor needs.

Here's another way to build on the idea: Don't listen alone. Bring along an expert "listener" or two from outside your industry. (See our discussion on "parallel engineering" in Chapter 3.) They will hear things differently from the way you do and point you toward simple opportunities you may otherwise miss.

Techniques for Increasing Your Fast-Fail Assets

On to the second quadrant. We love the fast-fail approach. It is fairly low risk—you don't spend much before you send the product out into the marketplace—and it has an extremely high potential reward as customers express exactly how they want you to alter it. Here are two techniques for implementing it:

Technique #1: Give it a shot. This is exactly what it sounds like. Come up with a crude version of the product you are thinking about introducing, rent a vacant store in the local mall, and ask people what they think. What would they add? What would they eliminate?

Technique #2: Partner. One of the best ways to test an idea is to find a company that can launch the concept regionally and would love to do so because it complements its services, products, or brand. You get in-market data and a partner who gives you momentum and future options. This technique allows you to quickly assess and profit from ideas you don't have time to manage. It even allows you to broaden your portfolio by investing in, or selling, great ideas that don't fit your model or brand.

Budgeting in Your Innovation "Portfolio"

To take our financial planning metaphor one step further, automatic "rebalancing" is important, too, when it comes to your innovation portfolio. Just like with your financial portfolio, when one portion of your assets becomes out of balance—stocks go on a nice run, and instead of making up two-thirds of your portfolio, they suddenly account for 75 percent—you readjust your holdings. It's no different when referring to innovation. Once an idea develops in the revolutionary or fast-fail quadrants, you probably want to move it to the evolutionary box after it grows and matures. In other words, the budget should be adjusted accordingly.

And the nice thing about approaching innovation this way is it makes the budgeting process substantially easier. There are fewer fights over funding someone's pet project, or chasing the current hot trend. Funding becomes strategic. You have your innovation asset allocation model, so to speak, and you divide the money up accordingly. This reduces stress at budget time by getting everyone thinking the same way about how to set priorities. It allows your team to stay focused on generating the right ideas and then implementing them, versus the hamster-wheel scenario of repeatedly guessing at the "how much should we spend?" question (and it also eliminates all the time wasted as people lobby for their favorite projects).

The idea of borrowing successful ideas from one place— a TV show that worked in Britain or a consumer electronics product that is all the rage in Japan and using it somewhere else (reworking that TV program for the U.S. market; modifying the consumer product to satisfy customers worldwide)—is a very common practice in innovation. We touched on this in Chapter 3. That's all you are doing here by borrowing the asset rebalance concept from financial planning.

We suggest you go rebalance your innovation portfolio once a year. This will allow you to manage your people, your money, and your ideas more intentionally. Although this may seem like a difficult task—and it may be the first time you undertake it—it can be done by asking your innovation team to report on all of the ideas/concepts in play. A suggested discussion would look as follows:

1. Meet with all the innovation leaders in your company.
2. Ask them to present or talk about each new product, service, or model concepts/ideas on which they are currently working.
3. Ask the question: How do we know our customers/consumers want this? Then dig into the specifics of how much qualitative/quantitative research supports the opinions. Sometimes the opinions are well founded, sometimes just a hunch.
4. Finally, ask this question: Is this something your company can easily do? If not, what stands in your way?

The answers to questions three and four will allow you to first place each concept in the proper quadrant because you will have a pretty good idea about true customer demand and your ability to execute.

For example, your answers will fall into one of the quadrants as defined by the general statements we offered you earlier:

- We know they want it and we know we can do it. (Evolutionary)
- We know they want it but we don't know (yet) how to do it. (Differentiation)
- We know we can do it, but don't know if anyone wants it. (Fast-fail)
- We don't know how to do it and don't know if anyone wants it. (Revolutionary)

Once you have your ideas organized into the four quadrants, you can easily see where your portfolio is out of balance and the map you've created will help you guide your team. There is even better news. We've never done this process for a client without finding initiatives that were worth doing but had somehow fallen off the radar of leadership. So chances are, you have a soon-to-be winning idea just under your nose but don't yet see it.

Many companies will disregard a product or service because it does not fit their financial model. For example, just because you sell products priced at $200 and up, don't kill an idea that will only sell for $20. You may be able to find a partner, who can sell millions of units, to give you a percentage of every sale. Apple gets a nice percentage of every app that you buy. If they were stuck thinking, "we make computers and sell them for thousands of dollars apiece, so why would we care about a 99 cent app?" they would be turning their backs on hundreds of millions of dollars.

You Must Remember This

1. **Are you in balance?** If you can't, off the top of your head, name where the ideas you are currently working on fit within your overall innovation strategy, something is terribly wrong. Use this chapter as a guide to sit down and plan out your innovation portfolio mix.
2. **Play matchmaker.** Certain people have certain skills. In the same way you divide your innovation portfolio, think about having people concentrate in the innovation quadrant that plays to their strengths.
3. **A good idea is a good idea even if it is not a good idea for you.** Farm out, sell, or joint-venture concepts you come up with that aren't necessarily a fit for your organization.

Coming Up Next

Now that you know how to construct your innovation portfolio, we are going to suggest you get some help—from extremely unlikely places—in doing so.

PART II

TOOLS AND TACTICS

CHAPTER 7

Getting Outside the Jar: How to Infuse Outside Experts into Your Innovation Process

It's sad but true: When it comes to how to create new products efficiently, you are probably too close to the problem. You know too much and, worse, you and your company are locked (perhaps unintentionally) into a fixed way of doing things. Bringing in outside experts—people not in your field—as you innovate will not only will give you a new perspective, but will also spark internal ideas as well.

"The significant problems we have cannot be solved at the same level of thinking with which we created them."
—Albert Einstein

We love this Einstein quote. And there is a great saying in the South that we think pairs with it perfectly: "You can't read the label when you are sitting inside the jar." From our experience that saying—like Einstein's—applies directly to your ability to innovate. If you have been with a company for more than six months, it is time you realize something: You're stuck in the jar. The way you think about new ideas is distorted by the corporate container you find yourself working within.

> Corporate culture can distort creativity without innovators realizing it. Luckily there are several telltale signs, and tips, to freshen up your perspective.

Said differently, you know too much. You know what your boss really wants. You know what your customer really wants. You know what you can actually produce and what you can't. You know what is legally possible. You know, you know, you know, you know.

As a result of everything you know, it is extremely difficult for you to see the priceless ideas that are all around you, ideas that will become the very new products and services your competitor will use to steal market share and give your boss a reason to question the effectiveness of your whole innovation strategy.

We know, we know. We can't be talking about you. (We had the same reaction ourselves, initially.) But if any of the following sounds familiar, you are in the jar, just like we were. (And fear not, there is a way out, which we will tell you about.) First, we want to give you some background on what is commonly called "practical wisdom." We hope it will help inform the discussion that follows on getting outside the jar.

Practical Wisdom

We love the quote "common sense is not that common" (attributed to Voltaire), because it is so often true when it comes to the innovation process. You can be so used to a certain way of thinking, doing things, and approaching problems, that you forget all about what Swarthmore Professor Barry Schwartz calls "practical wisdom"—looking for the simple (and profitable) solution that is right in front of you—but it happens all the time. Consider:

- Restaurateurs didn't start what we now know as McDonald's and Starbucks. Suppliers to those industries did.
- If ever there was a perfect entity to create overnight mail, it was the United States Postal Service. It didn't, of course.
- And simply search "Xerox Parc" on the Internet and look at all the stunning technology innovations that were developed there but were turned into products by someone else.

Practical wisdom is sucked out of our brains by the structures, policies, and procedures that we put into place in an attempt to make things more efficient, scalable, and safe. These policies are frequently tailored to a low common denominator because of sloth ("if I do what we have always done, I don't have to try something hard,") or because we simply don't trust people.

Practical wisdom is rooted in curiosity, in asking "why" or "why can't we. . ." (i.e., why do we need to be tethered to a telephone line to make a call, why can't we make a computer we can carry everywhere, etc.). What kills it is comments such as, "we have always done it this way," "we tried something like that before and it didn't work," or "they will never go for that." To guard against precedence becoming the enemy of innovation in your organization, try these four things:

1. Purge the "resistance to change" from positions of leadership. There is no easier way to show what the organization believes in.
2. Provide strategic balance between short-term pressures and long-term desired outcomes. Yes, you have

to hit your immediate goals—they *are* important—but your over-arching mission must always be viewed as what is essential. The "important" goes on your to-do list. The "essential" goes on your to-die-for list.

3. Raise the organization's level of consciousness through storytelling and transparency.

4. Once a quarter, take a process that you use every day and have someone less familiar with it go through it with an "internal process expert." Write it out step-by-step. Now, eliminate or question the steps that don't seem to add value. Chances are they were unintentionally added and don't belong.

If you do these four things, a meaningful progress toward innovation will prevail much sooner, rather than later. And it will help you get outside the jar which is limiting your creativity.

Reactions While Inside the Jar

You are in the jar when you hear any of the following reactions:

- "We've tested that idea. It didn't work."

  What idea exactly? People who are in the jar interpret ideas based on how they last saw them. In their minds, when they hear about a scooter, they think skateboard, not Segway. When they hear about an auction, they think Sotheby's, not eBay. Sometimes, they have literally judged an idea before it has been re-envisioned by the brilliant people around them and their experience blinds them to the possibilities of the future.

- Silence.

  When your team is trying to brainstorm new ideas, the room gets eerily quiet. The reality is that they are probably desperately trying to be creative but they keep seeing hurdles. They don't want to appear negative, so they decide to be silent and nod a lot.

- "Yes, but. . ."

  Trying to be polite, people will just "but" other people's ideas to death. ("It is a really interesting idea you are proposing, but it will never work because. . .") This is usually not about intent—they really want to be helpful—but they are too busy thinking about regulatory issues, manufacturing issues, political issues, budgetary issues, deadening their ability to be creative. Not only are they in the jar, but the lid is on really tight.

- An idea for (yet another) safe line extension.

  Line extensions and evolutionary innovation should be a large part of your plan, as we talked about in the last chapter. But when that's all your team is producing, it probably means they have lost the ability to recognize big ideas, or worse, they no longer have the fortitude to push the rock up the hill. Even when senior management begs for revolutionary thinking, they already see the outcome—"Let's just add a button, a flavor, or a perk and move on."

- "Jar-panese?"

  If you are often asked by really smart consultants or newcomers to your company what in God's name you are talking about, you're probably in the jar. Seems that after a few months in the jar together, we develop our own language. Often laced with industry-borne acronyms, this strange way of communicating seeps into our customer and client communications. These industry clichés keep our customers from recognizing great innovation.

  A few years back we scored big points with about 40 million customers when we convinced a client to change the last line on its monthly billing statement from "Account Balance" to "What you owe." You are surrounded by hundreds of similar examples.

If Your Client Has a Sense of Humor . . . try this. It works.

After our first meeting with a huge telecommunication client known for its industry-speak, we made a deal with them. Every time they used an abbreviation, code word, or tech talk as an adjective, noun, expletive, or other, the conversation would have to stop immediately and the person using the strange foreign language would have to formally explain exactly what they were talking about—in plain English.

Our team had fun with it. Some of them made small signs with question marks that they would hold up when a curious syllable was uttered. Trust us. We held up a lot of signs.

After a few meetings, the client became aware that they *really were* using a language that was gibberish to the rest of the world. And worse yet, it had insidiously seeped into all of their external communications. "Have we got a product for you, it's the XJZ343 mobility device." Making them aware of their strange internal language started a healthy pattern of listening and communicating that eventually reached their customers. They no longer use phrases like "the aforementioned rate payer" when communicating with customers. They now write "you." And what they were planning as introducing as the XJZ343, a really cool cell phone, was renamed for a Sci-Fi character before it reached the stores.

Stepping Outside

At the root of Zen philosophy is the ability to objectify your situation; to be able to step outside where you are and see it for what it really is—warts and all. So now that you see yourself in the jar, what do you do about it? Here are six simple tips:

1. **Get outside your office and act like an anthropologist.** Spend time with your customers and bring along an expert interpreter and a couple of members of your team. Compare notes; you will be shocked at how differently you all see situations.
2. **Be very careful about the language you use.** In this case, "voice of the customer" should be taken literally. Customers recognize, respond to, and build from their own words more than yours. So use their language when exploring insights, writing concepts, and introducing new products.
3. **Get experts from outside your industry to help you stay honest and see what is happening outside the jar.** Sure, you have smart people inside the jar. But so does the company down the street. Simply being smart doesn't give you an edge. It's just the price of entry if you want to come up with new products that will keep you ahead of the competition. To do that, you must move beyond smart.
4. **Find experts from the outside to be peers for the most influential experts on your team.** The challenge many of us have is our companies have team members who have built their reputations by demonstrating a deep understanding of the organization's most complex issues. These people are absolutely indispensable because when it comes to making an idea a reality, they have the time-tested wisdom to keep you from repeating mistakes. They are typically well-respected and often have nothing but good intentions. They often have a highly technical background, which means they can argue points you can't even begin to comprehend. And since you don't understand what they are so passionate about,

when they say "we can't do that," you are inclined to believe them.

This is where you must fight fire with fire. When we engage with clients, we immediately identify these thought leaders. They are usually notorious and easy to find. We then go outside the company to find a peer—someone with similar credentials but from a completely different industry. Ideally, we're searching for an expert that is delivering similar benefits. For example, we used a senior R&D expert from a paint company to help innovate insect control and deal with "Mr. Insect" at our client. Mr. Paint and Mr. Insect are both experts at working with chemicals. Both understand the legal issues that come with creating, distributing, and marketing chemical products. Both are passionate about innovating. We were able to get our client out of the jar simply by having Expert #1 share and challenge ideas with Expert #2. (It turns out, they got along great.)

5. **Infuse outside experts into every step of your innovation process.** They will see things you no longer do. Mike was shocked on a recent family canoe trip when his 12-year-old son found a frog at almost every portage. Up until then, Mike was concerned that the frog population was plummeting because he had not seen one in years. It turns out that he just doesn't see frogs anymore. Not sure why, but he just doesn't see them. However, 12-year-old boys still do.

This inability to see "frogs" may be more dangerous than you may suspect. As a leader you may have a bias or perhaps your brain has been trained to see and fall into certain patterns. Experts have a natural tendency to seek out information that confirms our hypothesis. Behavioral economists have a fancy term for this called, "confirmation bias"; meaning you naturally look for evidence that proves you are right. At Maddock Douglas we call this a "knower" mindset. It is not a good thing.

Pattern recognition can be the ultimate Achilles heal. Recently a research study of chess masters showed how their recognition of patterns could actually put them at a disadvantage when they played complete amateurs. You see, amateurs don't fall into expected patterns–they play by the seat of their pants. Unknowingly, the masters are confused by this because they presume their opponent is going to follow a certain pattern. This is *exactly* what happens in business when an inexperienced entrepreneur outplays a seasoned veteran. (See the McDonald's, Starbucks, and FedEx examples at the beginning of this chapter.)

We recommend you bring along outside experts to look for "frogs" in every step of the innovation process. When you do "ethnographic research," what you and I would call "going out into the field" to observe consumers as they go about their lives, bring along expert interpreters (an anthropologist; psychologist; a police detective, for example) and a couple members of your team. Compare notes; you will be shocked at how differently you all see the situation. When you do a segmentation study, have an outside expert (someone from another industry) interpret the data, she'll come to conclusions that your team will miss. When you brainstorm, look around the table. If you just see people you know from work, then you are unfortunately about to come up with the same old list of ideas. Yes, we're talking to you.

6. **Those outside experts should include consumers.** The end goal is to develop ideas that will sell. You need to follow the money. Let us reinforce a point we made in Chapter 3. What better way to bring your target and insights to life and develop ideas that will sell than to have your actual consumers—the people you want to buy what you plan to offer—in the room creating ideas and answering questions? If there is one kind of expert people tend to fail to include as

they go about changing their innovation process, this is it. Don't make this mistake. Include consumers. The best consumers to include are those who live a creative life. They tend to be more observant, more articulate, and more enthusiastic.

Connecting with Experts

The best, most innovative companies are discovering that expert connections are the new currency of innovation. A company's capacity to create industry-changing products and services is directly tied to its ability to forge connections efficiently between big brains both throughout the company and around the world. It turns out the old networking cliché is still true when it comes to innovation: It's not what you know, but who you know.

> The best, most innovative companies are discovering that expert connections are the new currency of innovation. It turns out the old networking cliché is still true when it comes to innovation: It's not what you know, but who you know.

Two of the benefits of infusing outside experts into your innovation process are obvious: You access additional expertise, and you generate momentum. (There is nothing like introducing your smart people to someone else's to spark all kinds of ideas.) But there are other benefits that get overlooked. For one thing, you gain objectivity. If you have been with a company for a while, you are not objective. Someone from the outside can say the atomic-powered buggy whip that the R&D people are in love with is simply not going to work. In addition, those outsiders can give you a different perspective you may desperately need.

Here's an example. For years oral-care companies have relied on dentists to help fill their innovation pipelines.

These companies cut their teeth (sorry!) in the professional channels, so naturally they believe dentists know more about oral care than anyone. After all, dentists spend their days talking to people about teeth, looking at teeth, thinking about teeth. So, if "four out of five" dentists think a new product idea is good, it must be, right?

Not necessarily. The world has changed. When you ask people about their mouths today, it turns out they don't talk much about cavities. They talk about sparkly teeth and fresh breath. The mouth is no longer just about dental health, it's about image. Stopping cavities is a must-have, not a game changer.

If you are looking to create innovation in oral care, you need to see it through the lens of aestheticians, stylists, and fashion experts. You need to forge relationships with people in all those fields to gain insights about what a toothbrush should deliver today.

The key, then, is you must really understand the needs of your consumer and what is it they want your product to do and then find experts who see these needs differently. Consider something as seemingly pedestrian as furniture polish. Think about what it does. It cleans, protects, and restores. Now, what other things do that? Well, lawn-care and skin-care products may be the first two that come to mind.

Armed with this realization, how do you gain another perspective? You could forge all kinds of formal relationships with other companies, but you don't have to do that. You can simply call someone at a lawn-care or cosmetic company and ask to pick their brains.

Everyone loves to be seen as an expert. Think about it. Isn't it flattering when someone asks you: "Can you help me?" Ask those people: "What opportunities do you see? What are the emerging trends?" You aren't a competitor, so odds are they will help, especially when you offer to share what you have learned with them. You want to create these kinds of partnerships to spur new thinking and draw connections to things you might not think are related.

Creating a Network of Experts

People get the idea of bringing in outside experts right away, but invariably they have questions. Three of the most common questions are:

1. *I like having the idea of differing perspectives, but I am afraid: What if these outside experts are going to steal my ideas in some form?*

   This is understandable but, remember, the people you are inviting in are not competitors. (An ethical competitor wouldn't come, even if they were invited by mistake.) The people you are bringing in as experts may do similar things—someone from the film industry is just as interested in fashion as you, the sweater manufacturers, are, but even with the rise of the *Transformers* movies, it is hard to see how they are going to benefit directly from the introduction of a new, form-fitting sweater. Have them sign confidentiality agreements—they won't hesitate for a second—and dive right in.

2. *I understand the benefit to me. But why would an expert want to be involved?*

   There are several reasons. Smart people like to solve challenges. Smart people like to work with other smart people; it sparks their thinking and builds their network. And, as we said, everyone wants to be considered an expert.

3. *Do I have to pay them?*

   Yes. Some will turn down your offer to pay them but most won't. How much they want for the consultation will depend on how much of their time you want.

Integration of the Left and Right Brain of an Organization

While you are bringing in outside experts, double check to see that you are not inadvertently limiting the creation of your best ideas internally. You could be doing that (accidently) by having your company rely too heavily on one type of thinking.

Typically, people fall into one of two camps: analytic or creative; rational or intuitive; logical or random; words or symbols; planning or impulsive, logic or feeling. We usually refer to this in shorthand as either left- (logical) brain thinking or right-brain (creative) thinking.

Obviously, no one camp is "correct," and, of course, everyone relies on *both* sides of the brain to function and think through everyday life decisions—big and small—but we all tend to rely more on one or the other (and very few people are exceptional at both).

This is an important distinction to consider because if we tend to rely on one kind of thinking over another, it means we have an innate bias, one that may not allow us to see obvious facts right before our eyes. As the old cliché goes, "if all you have is a hammer, then everything tends to look like a nail." We end up seeing things that just confirm the way we view the universe, and we filter out anything that conflicts with our world view because we have so much invested in it.

That's why we want to make sure that we fully draw on the left *and* right brains of our organization—more specifically, the left- and right-brain thinkers. That way you involve people who see data differently, make different assumptions, and ultimately give you a list of options that you would not have otherwise thought of.

So, how do you do it? We will give you specific ideas starting in the next paragraph, but all our suggestions have one thing in common: you need to make sure you have a balance of left- *and* right-brain thinkers in almost everything you do, especially if you're doing primarily a left-brain task or a right-brain task.

For example: If you are building an analytic segmentation model to identify the customers who have the highest long-term value to your company, bring in right-brain experts to tell stories of which segments they have seen based on their interactions with customers and time out in the field.

If you are doing an ideation exercise to try to come up with product ideas that can fill a hole in the marketplace, bring in left-brain thinkers to help map out a process of generating the best thoughts.

The key takeaway here, again, is that you are seeking a good balance of left- and right-brain thinkers throughout the innovation process. Not only will integrating the way everyone thinks lead to better ideas, but it will also satisfy the demands of upper management. The chief financial officer will be happy because you have done the left-brain homework to identify the potential size of a market opportunity, and the chief marketing officer will be delighted that you have creatively thought through all of the benefits and outcomes.

As long as we are throwing out similes in our search for ways outside the jar, let us give you another one.

Idea "Parents" Wanted

Our ideas are just like our kids. They deserve good parenting. What this means is the person who comes up with the idea should stick with it all of the way through introduction.

It sounds simple but as a rule, we as corporate executives ("parents") abandon our nurturing role too early turning over the idea to research and development and marketing and sales, once we think it is clear as it can be. And just like in any family ("company"), once the core set of executives (parents) is gone, the insight ("child") suffers. That's why we urge you to attend to the development of your idea at every step of the process.

The best companies establish a small, core innovation team—made up of all the key departments necessary to take a product from idea to marketplace (including finance and manufacturing people)—that stays with the insight all the way from discovery to launch, both internally and externally.

This team approach works for three reasons: It is small, focused, and empowered (by senior management because if they are not behind this, not surprisingly, it is not going to work well.)

If time is a problem—you can divide the parenting task into three parts, the three circles we talked about earlier. You can appoint an *insight parent* whose job is to make sure all ideas do, in fact, solve all the problems identified in the innovation process; an *idea parent* who guards to ensure that the concept remains true to the original intent, and a *communications parent* responsible for making sure that the communications link the insight and the idea.

If there does have to be a complete hand-off to someone who was not involved with the idea from the beginning, the later it occurs the better. To continue our analogy, turning an idea over to a "step parent" gets less dangerous the closer you get to launch.

The Role of Outside Experts in Building Your Innovation Portfolio

In Chapter 6, we explained the innovation portfolio model that we recommend to clients. Being in the jar has different ramifications, depending on which quadrant you are in. Still there are specific things you can do in each case. Refer to Figure 6.1 as we talk about what you can do, depending on where you are.

Evolutionary Innovation Quadrant

In this quadrant, you know what your customer wants and you know how to deliver it. The only risk is your people misinterpreting what your customers are seeking. We see this in insurance and other sales-driven industries where compensation models, or other factors, have companies trying to deliver a higher-priced product or something other than what the customer is requesting. (Salesmen who get an extremely high commission from selling things like variable annuities think they are a wonderful idea. Customers? Not always.) Here, an outside expert can keep you honest or tell you things that your sales team does not want to.

Differentiation Quadrant

In this quadrant, you know what the customer wants, but you just don't know how to deliver it. Here, it is not uncommon for your competitors to be trying to solve the exact same differentiation challenge. Outside experts can be a huge help in maximizing the uniqueness of the solution your team produces. Let's say you are working on an iPhone app intended to make it easier for a consumer to buy your product. Well, people from the travel industry have trained consumers in the best way to buy online. (When was the last time you used a travel agent?) You probably want to include someone from the travel industry in your ideation session. A person from inside your company may be so focused on reproducing the current experience or process that they may overlook the opportunity to improve it.

Revolutionary Quadrant

As we have said implicitly and explicitly throughout: Evolution comes from inside your halls; revolution comes from outside your walls. This quadrant is by definition dealing with things you don't know how to do and you don't know if anyone wants. You simply can't expect people inside your jar to deliver here. We recommend either:

a. outsourcing this quadrant completely,
b. setting up a separate innovation center, or
c. starting an "entrepreneur-in-residence" program.

You can coordinate all these things, but outside experts should drive the process.

Fast-Fail Quadrant

In this quadrant, you have an idea but don't know if anyone wants it. The obvious risk is that you drink your own Kool-Aid and go the way of the Iridium phone and create something really, really cool . . . that doesn't have a market. Use outside experts to help you find new channels, inexpensive ways to fail quickly, and—perhaps most importantly—tell you when to let a non-commercial idea die.

Conception Is a Matter of New Connections

People outside your jar have the ability to help you make connections you would otherwise miss. And new connections are at the heart of revolutionary innovation. That has been true throughout time. We love what Roger von Oech said about making connections: "Gutenberg connected the coin punch with the wine press to create the printing press. Mendel connected math with biology to create genetics. Fred Smith connected the hub and spoke idea of the wagon wheel to the U.S. Postal Service and created Federal Express. The roll-on deodorant was modeled after the ballpoint pen. Drive-in movies inspired drive-in banks. The common cocklebur inspired the design for the billion-dollar Velcro industry. You have the power to connect—use it!"

> People outside your jar have the ability to help you make connections you would otherwise miss. And new connections are at the heart of revolutionary innovation.

What to Tell Your Boss

Not surprisingly, your boss may be skeptical when you suggest introducing outside experts into the innovation process. He'll raise the issue of cost (since you have to pay these outsiders something for their time). He'll bring up the issue of confidentially (which won't be a problem since these people come from industries different than yours, and will sign non-disclosure agreements if you want). And he will ask the most fundamental question of all: "Why can't you guys do this all on your own?"

When he raises these questions—and others—you can say:

1. "We want to come up with something different than we usually do. If all we do is what we always have done, odds are nothing radically new is going to happen."

2. "We're stuck. We've exhausted all our options, and quite frankly everyone on the team is sick of looking at everyone else. We need new blood. We need to energize the groups."

3. "We need to broaden our footprint. Boss, you have charged us with something new, something that will get us into new markets. That's great. But by definition, no one here has done it before. We need people who have."

4. "We want to make sure we don't miss anything."

5. "It's cheap. These outside experts are helping us because they like dealing with new challenges. They are not charging us anywhere near their day rate."

You Must Remember This

1. **You are in a jar.** And that's okay. You have the necessary industry expertise to execute ideas. Just introduce some outside experts into the process, so you can come up with more ideas and better ones. Your competition is in the jar as well. This will keep you a step ahead.

2. **Any innovation effort can be enhanced with outside perspective.** Do what you do best, and let the outside experts supplement and improve it.

3. **Aim high.** If you have your senior-level people in the room, make sure your outside experts are also at a senior level.

Making sure you have (1) "outside-the-jar" thinkers as part of your process, who are (2) paired with left- and/or right-brain thinkers throughout, and (3) that "parents" are involved from inception to introduction into the market-place—and beyond, ensures the most success from idea to market. Otherwise, the more you bobble the "hot potato"— from person to person, group to group, and department to department—the higher and higher the likelihood of fail-ure. Why? Things get lost in translation. Motivations shift. New voices derail the outcome.

Coming Up Next

So, with some of the tools presented in this chapter in mind, let's look at what might seem to be an unusual place to try to innovate.

CHAPTER 8

Sustainable Innovation: Creating (and Profiting) from a Green, White Space

Q: "What is the newest innovation challenge going forward?"
A: "Finding an unmet need in the marketplace and offering
a product that fills it in an eco-friendly way."
Using a "green lens" can spur your thinking, keep your inno-
vation efforts extremely focused, and boost your bottom line.

A few years back, a conversation with one of our C-Suite clients started like many others, but it was the kicker that surprised us.

> Client: "We need $50 million in incremental growth from a new product or service within 18 months. It needs to strengthen our core MegaGalactic brand, and we must own the intellectual property because we don't want to be knocked off as soon as it hits the market. And oh yeah, the idea has to be *green*."

This request took place around the middle of 2005 and it served as our first real indication that Corporate America was (finally) getting serious about a favorite topic of tree huggers everywhere: going green. It also seriously changed our perspective on how your company and ours should develop new products, services, and positioning going forward.

> One of the newest challenges is finding an unmet need in the marketplace, and offering a product that fills it in an eco-friendly way.

Delivering on Needs *and* Making a Difference

In the world of innovation, a common goal has always been to find the "white space," which is another way of talking about the first circle of discovering unmet needs or untapped opportunities in the market. Spend enough time around effective innovators, and you'll find many think their ability to detect white space is their most important skill. And it is hard to disagree. There is nothing more crucial if you want to build an effective innovation engine. (That's why, as you recall, we said "market need" is the first thing you want to concentrate upon when you start to innovate.)

Fast forward to today. Business has discovered its customers will now pay for innovation that delivers on its needs *and* makes the world a better place. The examples range from necessities—extremely efficient toilets that use the absolute minimum amount of water, (some are in fact, waterless), to recharging devices for computers and cell phones that automatically shut themselves off once the charge is complete (to eliminate what is known as the "vampire draw"—the consumption of power when the device is off.)

The obvious difference between then and now is the importance of discovering the "green space." Finding it should become one of your key goals as you go about searching for huge market needs and the ideas that can successfully fill them.

Some of you may be rolling your eyes. We did too, at first. But times have changed, and looking at things through a green lens can no longer remain on your "we have to get around to doing this someday" list. In light of steadily increasing local, state, and federal regulations on the one hand and increasing demand from consumers for more green products (and more socially responsible companies) on the other, you need to do it today. If you wait, you risk losing your lead in the market, the confidence of your customer, or perhaps your job.

Let us stop right here to underscore what we are *not* saying. We are not arguing for going green because saving the environment is the right thing to do. (It is. But that argument isn't really effective with anyone who has to run a company, meet a payroll, and turn a profit.) We are arguing you should go green because sustainability is a key driver of innovation and carries a huge competitive advantage.

> Sustainability is a key driver of innovation and carries a huge competitive advantage.

Three Reasons to Find the Green Space

Let us tick off three reasons, starting with the intangible and working our way to the extremely tangible—and potentially even more profitable.

Reason # 1

It makes no sense to sail against the wind. You already know that all things being equal, consumers prefer green companies. And you probably understand that consumers are behind that governmental push we talked about toward mandating companies become more environmentally responsible. The upshot: You are going to have to go green. The only question is when. Our recommendation? It is always better to have the breeze at your back.

Reason # 2

Finding the green space can save you a lot of money.
Although some companies still see an eco-friendly overhaul
as an added cost of doing business without any substantial
financial benefit, that thinking is, for the most part, passé.
Adding a green tint to your business doesn't have to cost
more. In fact, in can be extremely profitable.

- Simply using fewer materials to make your products
  constitutes "going green," and also cuts costs.
- Moving production closer to where the products
  are consumed counts as another example of going
  green—because it reduces the environmental costs
  of transporting goods—and it definitely helps you
  attract more customers. You don't have to look any
  further than the whole movement toward eating
  locally grown foods.
- Recycling materials saves you money. Increasingly,
  municipalities are moving away from the concept that
  they will haul away all your waste for a flat fee and are
  adopting a model where you are charged (by weight
  or volume) for everything you throw away. The more
  you recycle, the less you are charged.

In fact, entrepreneurs are already acting on this insight.
For example, RecycleBank is in the business of motivat-
ing individuals to engage in positive sustainable actions
by giving reward points to incite behavioral change. For
instance, the more a consumer recycles, the more points
they receive that can be redeemed for merchandise.

In this business model, everyone wins: consumers get
points they can redeem at local and national retailers – the
more they recycle, the more points (and "real stuff") they
can get. Municipalities win because they save thousands on
landfill costs – and they become a "greener" city (mayors
love this!). Advertisers, retailers, and local merchants win –
by generating more consumers, buyers, and foot traffic.

RecycleBank wins, by sharing in the savings and generating foot traffic that yields significant revenue opportunities. And of course, the planet wins – with a literal doubling and tripling of recycling rates after RecycleBank moves into town.

Reason # 3

Finding the green space engenders a different way of seeing. For us, this ranks as the most exciting reason to go green. It gives you a new way of looking at the innovation process. Let's say you're in the flooring business. You think about competing on price, selection, kinds of materials, and all the other usual stuff. Now add a green lens. "Hmmm, what kinds of materials are easily renewable? Well, bamboo leaps to mind. I wonder if people would buy bamboo floors?"

The answer is "You bet." The material costs less than most kinds of wood and looks just as attractive (or more so.) It's a win for you, because you have a profitable new product to sell. And it's a triple win for consumers:

1. They end up with a product they like.
2. The product can be purchased at a lower price.
3. And, they get a product they feel good about because they made an environmentally smart decision (even if they didn't spend one single second thinking about the environment when they were considering bamboo. They just picked it because it was cheaper than the alternatives and would work well in the dining room.).

Another example: Outdoor "flooring" like decks made by companies such as Trex. As Trex points out on its website, its products are "made from about 50% recycled and reclaimed plastic and 50% reclaimed wood. These materials would otherwise go unused in landfills."

That's good, of course. But what appeals to most consumers even more is that Trex's materials last far longer than wood—which tends to rot—and don't need constant maintenance. (If you have ever stained a deck on a hot summer day, you understand the appeal of that.) And for those of us partial to walking around barefoot, the material doesn't splinter.

Why Wal-Mart Went Green

Next, if you still think this "green stuff" is too squishy, may we introduce you to "the (green) bully of Bentonville—because if Wal-Mart is going green, then you don't have any excuse.

Wal-Mart's vow to reduce energy in its stores is a green move. The company's trucks and other transportation vehicles now get 25 percent better mileage than they did five years ago and Wal-Mart is opening stores that are 25 percent to 30 percent more energy-efficient and, as the company points out on its website, will "produce up to 30% fewer greenhouse gases."

Stating a belief we share, Wal-Mart announced: "We know that being an efficient and profitable business and being a good steward of the environment are goals that can work together." Going forward the company's goals are: to be powered 100 percent by renewable energy, to create zero waste, and "to sell products that sustain people and the environment."

We believe Wal-Mart took on green because they knew it would buff up a corporate image that had taken a beating. But they also did it because they knew it was good for the bottom line. Wal-Mart really nailed their green space. They knew everyday consumers—the ones who couldn't afford a Prius—still wanted to make a difference. And Wal-Mart knew they had the muscle to pressure suppliers into creating the green products that those consumers wanted.

So Wal-Mart gave people affordable, more environmentally conscious products. They also made their entire operation leaner—from making their stores energy efficient to changing the way their trucks were packed and driven.

They called all this "Eco-Efficiency." And at every step, they turned it into bottom line savings and profit.

Why did we spend so much time talking about Wal-Mart? Well, if a company that is known for being "hard-nosed" thinks green is good, it may very well be. Speaking of hard-nosed, you probably know that *Fortune* magazine named former GE chief Jack Welch "the CEO of the 20th Century." But for all the accolades he received throughout his career, those handing out plaudits missed a huge one: He was the King of Green. After all, Six Sigma, the management style he championed, is all about getting leaner: reducing steps, costs, and materials. Lean is green.

Steps toward Integrating Sustainability into Your Innovation Process

We believe integrating sustainability into the everyday fabric of the way your company operates spurs long-term growth, and the data bears us out. The following is from a study done by The Economist Intelligence Unit and Deloitte: In the race for market leadership and differentiation, forward-thinking companies are looking to green innovation as a key to future profitability—and also as a shield against commoditization.

> "The markets agree. . .companies that embrace sustainability have achieved the highest share price growth over the past three years, whereas companies with the worst performance focused less on sustainability."[1]

Today and for the foreseeable future the creation of sustainable products, services, and business models that respond to consumers' unmet needs will drive profit. Companies that do good will, in turn, do well. And companies that refuse to

---

[1]Deloitte White Paper: "The Green Gap: Avoiding Pitfalls on the Sustainability Path to Shareholder Value" January, 2009.

comply with environmental standards and respond to consumer concerns will see punitive results.

If you are convinced that going green is good business, what do you need to do? The answer has three parts:

- Figure out where you are today with green.
- Determine how to improve (both in short and long term).
- Find where the green space opportunity is for you, based both on what your consumers want and where it fits in with your brand. Then go grab it.

Next, we describe how these steps can play out in practice by offering the four categories most companies find themselves in when related to green.

Where You Are and What You Should Do

The odds are that, when it comes to green, you can classify your company in one of four categories:

Bashful	Leader
Laggard	Lucky

We will go through each—and then prescribe what you can do to improve or make the most out of where you are.

1. Is your company just getting started with green (or hasn't done a thing)? Then you fall among the Laggards.

The good news is you have no place to go but up. But your Laggard status also means, of course, that you trail competitors who have already taken steps. And you're doomed to grapple awkwardly with all the new regulations coming out. (It is always far better to control the agenda than to let it control you.) Our advice: Look beyond where you are today, to where you want to be tomorrow. Be transparent and get started. Say (both internally and externally) something like, "We haven't done much up until now, but we will soon do X, Y, and Z." Develop short-term and long-term green visions and corresponding plans for prioritized actions; begin a deliberate transition to green consumer-facing innovations—that is, tell the consumer on your website, packaging, and the product itself—what green actions you have taken—as well as measurable internal practices; and then execute. Obviously this should come from the top of the organization. So hand this book to the CEO when you are done with it. (Better yet. Buy him his own copy.)

2. Has your company been actively but quietly working on green for years? Then you are a member of the Bashfuls.

We understand why you didn't want to toot your own horn. You figured, correctly, greening was the right thing to do, so you just did it and didn't expect accolades. Besides, in the past, so much noise has surrounded the green movement that it was often risky to "throw in" with the rabble rousers and all the folks yelling "look at me," even though many of them hadn't done very much. Our advice: Get noticed and get focused. Your modesty, while admirable, is potentially self-defeating if consumers don't know what you stand for, let alone what green offerings you have. You want the industry to see you as a leader in the category—because you are.

If you're wondering how to reposition yourself without being accused of bragging, take a look at what Hanes[2] has done with its website. The clothing company has put its innovative products, packaging, and communications into a larger context. The site is educational—you'll read that some 30 percent of the energy Hanes uses comes from renewable sources—and relevant to customers—"did

---

[2]Full disclosure: Hanes is a client. But we aren't associated with their website.

you know 90% of the energy used in a warm cycle goes to heating the water? Get your laundry just as clean and make the planet happy by running a cold water cycle." You don't end up thinking Hanes is being boastful—just being transparent and consistent with the company's long-term vision and values as you can see from the following descriptions they offer their customers online (http://www.hanesgreen.com/environmental-responsibility.html):

Hanesbrands has quietly become a leader in energy management and aspires to be an international apparel industry leader in overall environmental responsibility and stewardship. This effort is more than a commitment; it is a major business strategy for our success. Using sustainable practices and conserving natural resources to mitigate our environmental footprint and reduce costs is one of Hanesbrands' core efforts to create value for our company, our investors, our consumers, our employees and our communities. We have made significant progress in our efforts over the past few years, but we have the potential to achieve much more and are mobilizing to do so.

Our big brands and large-scale global supply chain—primarily plants that we own—not only give us a competitive advantage in business, they also allow us to make meaningful contributions to environmental stewardship faster than many of our peers. We're doing our share to address global climate change and can do so effectively because, unlike many other apparel companies, we produce the significant majority of our products in plants that we own and operate. We are systematically assessing our impacts on the environment and have identified a broad set of areas to address. In addition to energy and carbon management, we recognize the importance of managing the other impacts of our operations, notably water use, wastewater, solid waste, raw materials, chemical use, and product packaging.

The point here: Showcase green innovations as a core business priority and create ongoing dialogue with the public to openly share your commitment to sustainability.

3. **Has your company been perceived as green even though you're not actively doing much? Then you are one of the Lucky Dogs. But you should anticipate that your luck is about to run out.**

Certain companies (and we won't name them) are perceived as trendy, cutting edge, cool, hip, design-focused, and so on, and consumers tend to provide them with a "halo" that extends to everything they do. As a result, consumers just assume they are leaders in green, even if they are not.

Our advice: Get serious. First, figure out why consumers are giving you credit for things you haven't done. Then actually do those things, and more. The opportunity for you to get new green innovations into the portfolio mix quickly and get them to market is tangible. Your audience already expects it.

What approach should you take? Simultaneously and transparently, identify and disclose what you plan to do over the short and long term. If you don't, you could face a huge backlash once consumers find out you have not behaved the way they thought. You may have millions of dollars' worth of consumer goodwill pulled off the table should you find yourself "outed" by the media or a competitor.

4. **Has your company been actively and openly setting the standard for green in your industry? If yes, you are clearly in with the Leaders.**

Our Advice: Get further ahead, now! Capitalize on your green leadership position by exposing the green disparity between you and everyone else. Enhance your green innovation portfolio of offerings to deliver on today's consumer demands and future market demands. You want to be known for your big-picture, whole-systems thinking when it comes to green initiatives.

Actions Speak Louder than Words

We want to stress that change comes from action, not a soap box. For any green puritans reading this who may feel tempted to connect our proposals with something other than tangible, meaningful progress for the desired outcomes of the "movement," we suggest that you reconsider. Hectoring is not helpful here.

Common sense will tell you why. What will create action soonest and most effectively is aligning consumer purchasing behavior with corporate behavior, not guilt and condemnation. Conscious capitalism works, if action is the desired outcome. Use the carrot more than the stick. The soap box (or ranting or embarrassing people and corporations) may have worked for raising awareness, but it isn't going to create the outcome you want in regard to action. What will is creating the self-funding sustainability initiatives we are advocating here.

One last point: In the United States, we have the great displeasure of watching bipartisan bickering slow even the most obviously needed initiatives. (Is any rational person going to argue we need to reform the way we provide health care, tax people, handle immigration, educate our children? . . . Unfortunately the list is a very long one.)

The same thing is happening with green initiatives. Often, the immediate reaction of many is to point out what is *not* working (or what won't work). While we agree that everyone, including our biggest corporations, could do more, let's not lose sight of one big point. It is actually becoming more profitable for them to see things through a green lens, and consequently good things are happening. So yes, let's all push companies to keep it real, but let's recognize and reward them when they start taking steps in the right direction. It's time to let go for a better grip.

We encourage every company, and every individual associated with creating the new, to look at innovation through an additional lens—one that is green. It can help you come up with a broader range of profitable products and services to make your customers happy.

Everyone should include green initiatives in their innovation process. It can help you develop a broader range of profitable products and services and, at the same time, make your customers happy.

The 5 Cs of Sustainable Innovation

What will it take for you to innovate successfully in the new green, white space? We have reduced the answer to five words. You need to be: competitive, consumer facing, core, conversational, and credible.

Competitive

All other benefits being equal today, sustainability differentiates and provides a tangible competitive advantage. Tomorrow, that will not be the case, consumers will expect that your product will be the best and most innovative and be sustainable. And they won't pay a premium for green. They will simply expect it. This will be no different than what happened in any other industry. Shoppers want the best price and the best service. They won't pay a premium for service. They expect it. Car buyers want cars they can afford and ones of the highest quality. It will be no different here.

Consumer Facing

Not sure what to do first? Look at what the consumer is looking at. You want to get the most benefit out of your new sustainability initiatives by making them something the consumer will see (on your stationary, packaging materials, website, and the product itself). Consumer-facing changes will have the most immediate impact on public perception and, potentially, financial performance. When consumers said they wanted a green cleaning product, Arm & Hammer pointed out in all their communications that their baking soda had been a green cleaner since 1846. Home run.

Core

Tying sustainability to a brand's core business is another way to ensure it resonates with consumers. If your brand sells hamburgers, its sustainability has to be about hamburgers (e.g., organic beef, recycled wrappers). Don't do something that is unrelated to what people know you for, or they won't reward your efforts. Car brands must focus on making more fuel-efficient, cleaner cars—not saving the rainforest. If you do something that is unrelated to your core business, you risk alienating or confusing your consumers—at best. Yes, you want to be a good corporate citizen, but your actions should be related to your brand for clarity's sake.

Conversational

Sustainability branding is more effective as a two-way conversation rather than one-way communication. Honesty and transparency will go a long way with consumers. Disclosing what you're doing well and what you could be doing better will instill trust. Think of Patagonia's Footprint Chronicles, an online tool that helps consumers understand Patagonia's strides in making their shirts and pants more sustainably . . . and also lets them see the environmental shortcomings of Patagonia's products as well. This kind of disclosure creates trust, and trust breeds loyalty. Inviting consumers to participate in a conversation about your process will further strengthen the brand/consumer relationship.

Credible

Sustainability strengthens brands. But greenwashing (the term used when a company spends more time/money/ effort talking about how it is "green" than actually being green), even if unintended, damages them. The key is sequence. As long as sustainability efforts are in place, before being announced, they will be viewed as credible. And proven, objective credibility paired with innovation and communication is the key to sustainable brand success. And proven, objective credibility, when paired with innovation that excites, and communication that clarifies and engages, is the key to sustainable brand success.

> Sustainability strengthens brands.

Corporations continue to frame the story of sustainability—the idea of integrating environmental concerns into their business strategy while maintaining economic competitiveness—as a problem they want to make go away. In short, they limit their thinking to mitigation (the act of minimizing loss or damage).

That casts sustainability in an unnecessarily negative light. This encourages a defensive, unimaginative approach to innovation; a defensive stance which dampens innovative thinking, progress, and profit. That is just wrong. Instead of thinking about eliminating a negative—be it an environmental/sustainability concern or anything else—we always need to think bolder.

For example, the BP spill in the Gulf in 2010 highlighted for the umpteenth time that countries need to do something about their dependence on oil. True, the U.S. relationship with oil has spurred unprecedented innovation—thank you, Mr. Ford. But committing to new sources of energy would unleash an equally impressive wave of thinking.

On the one hand, it's easy to understand a collective hesitation to do anything radical. It satisfies a very human need for comfort and certainty. But when business leaders dare to chart a bold course of eco-innovation, the results can be exhilarating. You only need to look as far as Dupont's remarkable green transformation—the company has gone from being the scourge of environmentalist to a poster child for what to do right—and GE's Ecomagination, a business initiative designed to meet customers' demands for more energy efficient products "and to drive reliable growth for GE."

You Must Remember This

1. **Kermit was right.** It has been more than 40 years since Kermit the Frog first sang "it's not easy being green." It still isn't easy, but it is now mandatory.
2. **Green is the color of money.** As Wal-Mart and others are proving, going green is (extremely) profitable.
3. **Actions speak louder . . .** than any possible pronouncement you can make in this space.

Coming Up Next

Want to know if your innovation effort has a legitimate chance to succeed? So did we. That's why we created the prediction tool that you will read about in Chapter 9. (Hint: It works really well.)

Introducing "The Innovation Power Score"—A Method for Measuring the Potential of Your Innovation

We have created a simple way to measure how well you are doing in executing against the three interlocking circles that make up innovation—need, idea, and the communication that links the two. It is called The Innovation Power Score and it helps you to score each circle on its own merits, as well as the process as a whole. It will give you a solid idea of your chances of success, even before you launch your product or service into the marketplace.

"If you cannot measure it, you cannot manage it."
—Peter Drucker

Peter Drucker's quote is right, of course. If you can't track your innovation efforts, there is no way you can expect to manage them properly. That's why we invented the Innovation Power Score (IPS) as a methodology that not only measures how well you're doing—or not doing—when it comes to your innovation efforts, but it is implicitly prescriptive as well. It allows you to tell at a glance what part of your innovation efforts need to be improved.

Not surprisingly, we are very proud of it. But, before you can start measuring anything, you need to know what you're measuring. That seems obvious. Yet we are constantly surprised as we work with some of the world's largest companies by how varied their definition of innovation is. We have seen a few companies that don't have a working definition of innovation at all (management just assumes that every employee knows what innovation means to the firm and that the explanation they have come up with on their own is the same for everyone else). And, we have even seen companies that have multiple written/documented definitions that vary depending on who your boss is, or what division you work for (and the divisions never thought to synchronize or coordinate their definitions).

How can you expect to get your chief financial officer to support (or approve additional money) for your innovation efforts, if you cannot define what innovation is? And here is an even more basic question: How can you know how well you are doing, if you can't even describe what you are doing?

The answer to these questions is: You can't.

> The Innovation Power Score allows you to spot problems quickly and correct them.

In creating the IPS we wanted to make sure everyone was on the same page. Our definition of innovation which you read about in Chapter 2 (refer to Figure 2.1), declared that innovation has three inter-related parts:

1. The market insight/need;
2. The idea for a product or service that addresses that need, and;
3. Creating a communication that links the two.

As we mentioned at the start of the chapter, the really nice thing about the Innovation Power Score is that you can not only measure your overall performance but measure how well you are doing in each of the three circles. Let's begin with the insight/need and see how it works.

The Insight Score

Not surprisingly, the first component of the IPS is the "Insight Score." As we said in Chapter 3, the innovation process starts with finding unmet needs in the marketplace.

> If your IPS score is low, odds are the need you have discovered isn't big enough.

There's another reason we are starting the discussion here. Once you have a list of insights, the questions become: "Which ones do I focus on? Which one or two are the most relevant for my core target audience? And which ones solve the biggest problems that they have?" No business has the capacity, budget, or time to create products or services for every one of the needs you will discover. And no business or brand should, or can, be all things to all consumers or customers. You want to solve the biggest possible problems that fit with what your organization does for a living, in order to make your customers happiest (and make you the most money in the process). The Insight Score will identify where you should focus.

Let's see how it works.

Components of the Insight Score

When it comes to identifying potential needs, the Insight Score has five components and you need to look at all five.

Confirm the Tension **First, you must make sure that the problem you have observed is a bothersome one in the eyes of consumers or customers.** Going back to our formula for capturing insights that we talked about in Chapter 3 . . .

> I (insert "fact" here) because (insert "why" here) but (insert "tension" here)
>   . . . we see that what you are actually doing is measuring the tension.

Let's take some sample observations, made by a large Consumer Packaged Goods (CPG) company, which identified a very valuable consumer segment within the Baby Boomer population (those 78 million consumers born between 1946 and 1964) who love to cook at home and are very involved in their food. For illustrative purposes, let's just call this segment the "Empowered Trailblazers."

Why was the CPG so interested in this cohort, other than the pure size and purchasing power of this market? Because this specific target segment (unlike many of their peers) were very involved in the food they ate. Food was more than mere "sustenance." To this specific sub-segment of Boomers, food served many functions. Preparing meals from scratch was perceived as an antidote to growing old—they could choose exactly what healthy food to consume. It was a way to say "I love you," to the person they were cooking for. And it was a glue for social connectedness. (Just to name a few.) Food clearly was more than just "fuel" and they were prepared to pay a premium to cook and eat the way they wanted.

As we talked with these empowered trailblazers, we heard lots of needs the CPG could potentially solve for. Among them:

> "I like to make dinner for my family because it's part of my role as nurturer, but I could use some help making sure we're all getting the nutrients and vitamins we need to stay healthy."

"I love cooking because it shows my family how much I love them, but I wish there was a simpler way to prepare fresh, healthy food every day."

"I like to make dinner when I invite my friends or family because it is much more personal and intimate than going out, but I'm concerned that my cooking will not measure up to my guests' expectations."

"I like to cook for myself because this way I know all the ingredients that are healthful but I don't know what foods help prevent or counteract what specific health ailments."

Having heard these comments, we began to test these insights. We asked a large sample of empowered trailblazers—questions like these can be asked face to face online, or over the phone—to describe how much these problems bothered them. We wanted to quantify what they felt, so that we would have some objective way to compare their answers. So we asked respondents to rate each "problem" this way: "On a five-point scale where five is 'describes completely' and one is 'does not describe at all,' please tell me the degree to which each of the following statements describes you."

The scale looked like this:

Does not describe me at all.

Slightly describes me.

Somewhat describes me.

Describes me very well.

Describes me completely.

To keep the scoring simple, we converted it to a scale of 0 to 100: the answer "describes me perfectly" gets a 100, "describes me a great deal" gets a 75, "somewhat describes me" was a 50, "describes me slightly" was 25, and "not at all" was a zero.

Determine the Frequency of the Tension   **Second, make sure that the problem occurs with some frequency**. If the tension, the problem you are trying to solve for, only happens every couple of years this may not be a market need you want to hang your hat on. It *could* be worthwhile if the problem— your laptop gets the "blue screen of death," (i.e., it turns into a six pound paperweight—occurs only once every three or four years, however, you "would pay anything" to get it working again when it happens. But there are not a lot of tensions that fall into this category. So you have to assess how frequently the "problem" you have discovered happens.

For example, in our study of Baby Boomers who like to cook at home, we found two problems—"I am afraid that my cooking won't measure up to my guests' expectations," and "I wish there was a simpler way to prepare fresh, healthy food"—that were both extremely "bothersome." They both were perceived by many to describe them very well.

But the "simpler way to prepare fresh, healthy food" problem occurred almost every day (just about every time this person cooked for his/her family) while the other concern only happened once a month (when they entertained). You don't want to rule out creating a solution for an infrequent problem (like cooking for friends twice a month) at this point. But you do want to be aware that it may be difficult to charge enough to justify solving it.

The specific survey questions that are used to measure frequency will of course vary depending on your specific category/industry or product/service, and that's okay. You just need to make sure you use a comparable scale across "problems" so that you can compare findings over time. That's why you want to ask exactly the same questions and provide the same potential responses every time so you can compare the answers head-to-head.

What Tension Is Most Important Third, figure out which *one* problem is the "most important." Which tension is the *one* that consumers wished would just "go away"? Although we have (in component number one) the absolute rating in terms of its "bothersomeness" for each insight statement, this is a second level of consideration that should be captured. For any given tension you want to discover what percent of your target segment said it was the number one or the "top" problem they wanted resolved.

In addition, this question often functions as a tie-breaker. That is no small thing. Just about every marketer can cite several cases where the differences among various "needs" tested were statistically insignificant. It is good to have something to look at to help you decide which way to go should that be the case.

Confirm the Tension Is Unresolved Fourth, confirm that the problem or need is not being addressed well by a product or service already out there. We worded that carefully. It is possible that there are products or services in the marketplace designed to deal with the need you have discovered. That's okay. The Coca-Cola Co. did not invent diet soft drinks and Lowe's did not invent the big box home improvement store. While ideally you would like to face no competition in the marketplace, you still can do well if existing products are not doing a good job of resolving the problem you have uncovered.

In our earlier example, we found that the friction surrounding the statement, "I am afraid that my cooking won't measure up to my guests' expectations," was being somewhat addressed by advice in cookbooks and also by "entertainment shows" on the Food Network and elsewhere. However, neither was perceived to be doing a very good job at addressing the need. As for the other problem related to "knowing what foods help prevent or counteract what specific health ailments" the research at the time showed it was not being addressed at all. In cases like these, one way to discover that is to ask an open-ended question such as: "You mentioned earlier that you were concerned that your cooking was not measuring up to your guests' expectations. Could you please list any products or services you might have used or have heard of that might help you resolve this problem?" If you have done research, and are aware of potential solutions to the problem that are already available, you could ask a follow up question like: "How well do you think X product does in addressing your need?" giving your target five answers—ranging from "completely" to "not at all"—to choose from.

Will *Customers* Pay to Solve the Tension   Finally, make sure you're looking for a problem that customers are open to paying something to resolve. You are not trying to figure out yet what to charge. The questions you ask here are less a measure of identifying *how much* they'd be willing to pay for a solution to the problem and more of a "check" to make sure customers are at least not resolutely opposed to paying anything. For example, in a study for a utility company that we did, we found that customers were adamantly opposed to paying anything to resolve power outages. ("I'm not willing to pay a penny. Problems should be fixed and as soon as possible. The price of getting the power back on is already included in my bill." That was the response we heard over and over.)

In our Baby Boomer study, the Empowered Trailblazer target was very open to paying something to ensure that "their guests' expectations were met" when they entertained. (That's how you ask the question, by the way: "How open would you be to paying for a solution that eliminated this problem?" With the choices being "completely open," "very open," "somewhat open," "slightly open," and "not at all.") However, none of the ideas that were generated—such as a 99 cent app available via cell phone—were ever at a price point around which the client could build a business.

The company, could, of course, decide to provide the service and not charge for it. But while there are obviously good reasons for sometimes providing a product or service for free—increased awareness, building loyalty, and so on—if you go too far down this road, you go broke in a hurry.

■ ■ ■

The Insight Score has to take these five components into account. Each component is quantitatively measured and scored (in the method we talked about when we discussed the first component) on a scale of 0 to 100. Then, you add up all the scores and divide by five (the number of questions). This will give you a score of somewhere between 0 and 100 and make it easy for you to compare at a glance the various needs you have uncovered.

Again, it is too early in the process to commit to going forward or killing an idea. But if you are not scoring in the top 25 percent of the IPS database or, if you have existing data points within your company, and you are not scoring in the top tier of winning insights you have tested in the past, warning bells should go off. The shorthand of looking at this: You are looking for a passing grade of 70 or above.

The Idea Score

The second dimension is the idea: The product or service designed to solve the need that you have discovered. We talked previously (see Chapter 7) about the absolute need to infuse an outside perspective in the ideation process. But let us underscore the point here. If you and your colleagues outnumber the outsiders who are ideating in the room, the likelihood of coming up with a breakthrough, industry-changing idea is pretty small. But assuming that you've infused outside experts, and you've come up with what you think is an industry-changing idea, then the questions at this stage are:

- How big an idea is this?
- How can we quantify it?
- How much top-line revenue will it bring into our organization?

Components of the Idea Score

The Idea Score can help you answer the previous questions. It, too, has five components.

Does the Idea Help Resolve the Tension   **First, the idea for the product or service has to be perceived as helping to solve the problem.** It must be seen as specifically addressing the need you have discovered. That is, regardless of how much the product is liked (which is always something you want to measure/capture; and you see how to do that in a minute) you also need to assess whether it is seen as helping to solve a concern your target has. This is measured using a five-point scale where five is "resolves this problem completely" to one, "does not resolve this problem at all."

Let us show you how this could play out in practice. In the Baby Boomer study, one (of the hundreds) of potential concepts generated was the thought of creating an online cooking class. You would log on at the appointed hour and cook live with an instructor via an Internet hook up. Its interactive nature would allow for communication among other participants, as well as with well-known chefs and approachable celebrities. Although the idea was specifically generated to address the need for "a simpler way to prepare fresh, healthy food every day," it didn't resonate with the target market. (They did say it could fulfill the much more minor need they had for "learning how to cook better.") Although the idea was generally well liked by the target, it did not serve a big enough need—most of the target was fairly comfortable with their ability to cook—so we eventually passed on the idea.

Is It Unique   **Second, the idea needs to be perceived as being different from any other product or service currently available.** As you know, it is very difficult to get people to shift their routines, or change what they buy on a regular basis. If your idea is the same as what is already out there, or even if it is slightly better, the odds are people are *not* going to abandon what they have. That's why one way we define successful innovation is in terms of creating industry-changing ideas—and those are not typically the "me too" products (nor line-extensions). For a new product or service to make a splash and meet our definition of innovation standards, it has to be seen as different and/or extremely better than the existing alternatives.

Here again you can use a five-point scale where five is "totally unique" from anything currently available, four is "very unique," three: "somewhat unique," two "slightly unique," and one is "not at all unique/different."

Does the Target Want to Know More   **Third, the idea has to make the customer or potential consumer immediately want to learn more about it.** This is particularly relevant for service concepts which tend to be more complicated to explain and/or have a multi-step buying process. For example, if you are in the financial services industry, you want your idea for a new type of annuity, or an innovative mortgage insurance product, to be so compelling that the potential customer immediately seeks out a broker or agent.

Each idea is rated on a five-point scale where five means you "definitely want to learn/find out more about this service" and one means you are "not at all interested in finding out more." And the scores are totaled exactly the same way as before. A "definitely want to learn more" gets a 100. "Not interested at all" gets a zero.

Do They Want to Spread the Word **Fourth, the idea (or product or service) should trigger a desire in your target segment to want to tell others about it.** If we want the new idea to have an impact in the market, it needs to create buzz. It should generate an excitement level such that it makes your target say to their friends or co-workers, "Hey, did you guys hear about this? We've got to try it." For people who need to be in touch at all times it was Google Voice. It's a single phone number that rings on every phone you own, and if you don't answer, sends transcribed messages to your email address. For the hard core athletes, it was Vibram's five-finger shoes ("the barefoot alternative") or most recently, among the fashionistas, it is Burberry's website that lets you buy high couture right off the runway. You don't have to wait for the merchandise to be shipped to stores.

The higher the idea scores on this measure, the more likely it is to make a market impact. Although line extensions and me-too products can survive by just grabbing a few share points, truly innovative products generate excitement and word of mouth and change industries. To find out if you have one of those game-altering concepts, each idea is measured using a five-point scale where five means it is "extremely likely" you will tell your friends about the idea, four means "it is very likely" you will, three means it is "somewhat likely" you will, two is "slightly likely," and one means "not at all likely."

Will They Buy It **Fifth, we, of course, want to know whether the target customer thinks they would purchase the idea or service we have come up with.** The shorthand way of expressing this is, "what is the purchase interest," or, "what is the purchase intention." Although many companies use this primarily (or solely) to rank or measure their new product or service ideas, we believe that is far too simplistic. You need to ask the other four questions we have talked about to get a complete picture of what people think of the idea.

Still, purchase interest is important. We like to use the Juster Purchase Scale, which gives 11 possible answers to the question "would you buy this product?" You will notice it employs both words and numbers to capture the information, so both left- and right-brain people are completely comfortable in answering. The answers people get to choose from are:

Certain that I will buy (that is, 99 chances in 100)

Almost certain I will buy (that is, 90 chances in 100)

Very probable that I will buy (that is, 80 chances in 100)

Probably will buy (that is, 70 chances in 100)

Good possibility I will buy (that is, 60 chances in 100)

Fairly good possibility I will buy (that is, 50 chances in 100)

Fair possibility I will buy (that is, 40 chances in 100)

Some possibility I will buy (that is, 30 chances in 100)

Slight possibility I will buy (that is, 20 chances in 100)

Very slight possibility I will buy (that is, 10 chances in 100)

No chance I will buy (that is, 0 chances in 100)

Once you have the five scores, add them up and divide by five. This will allow you to easily rank your ideas from high to low and help you identify which have the greatest potential to be industry changing. As a further check, all the Idea Scores can also be compared to your historical norms (i.e., other ideas that you had tested in the past, assuming you had tracked their success).

The Communication Score

As we discussed in Chapter 5, communication is what connects the insight/need to the idea.

Components of the Communication Score

The right communication delivers successfully against these five components.

Do They Get It   **First, the insight/idea must be easy to understand.** If your innovation is something new, you need to explain it in a way that people instantly "get." A few years back Chrysler, Ford, and General Motors began running aggressive sales campaigns based on a new complicated pricing model based on—among other things—their actual cost, plus the absolute minimum mark-up necessary to cover the cost of getting the cars to their dealers, the advertising cost per vehicle (their total advertising budget divided by the number of cars they expected to sell), plus the "hold back," a percentage (usually 1 percent to 3 percent of the sticker price) that manufacturers rebate to dealers. How did the car companies communicate all of this complicated math? They had one of their employees look into the camera and say "for the next month, if you buy one of our cars or trucks, you will pay what we (employees of the car company) pay."

The communication worked. Sales soared.

Does It Say Something New   **Second, the insight/need has to be perceived as saying something different.** The consumer has to react to your message with "Hey, there is something out of the ordinary here, and I'm intrigued." The classic example of this is the Intel Inside ad campaign. Prior to those now-ubiquitous ads, if you mentioned the word "microprocessor" to consumers, odds were you would get a totally mystified stare in return. Few consumers knew anything about the processor even though it was the "brain" that powered the computer. "Intel inside" gave them new information, and in the process got Intel out of the commodity chip business. All of a sudden, they were selling a branded product. Michelin provided new intriguing information with its ads that suggest the safety in an automobile starts with how good your tires are. The fundraising technique ("text 90999 to send $10") to help earthquake victims in Haiti let people know their cell phone could be a payment device.

Does the Idea Come Across in a Fun Way   Third—and, we love this one—the communication has to be enjoyable. It's got to be fun. It's got to be something you want to hear, listen, or read about again. One example of that is the Dove Men Care ad that first ran during the 2010 Super Bowl. It's a funny spot where a man sees his whole life, from the time he was a swimming sperm until he becomes a father of three, pass in front of him while lyrics (set to the William Tell Overture) explain what is going on. The point of the ad? A real man is comfortable in his own skin. The spot scored extremely well when we tested the communication component. Other examples of commercials that deliver against the enjoyable requirement: Dos Equis beer spots with the "most interesting man in the world" and the ads for Old Spice featuring the frequently bare-chested man who begins every spot by saying "ladies. . .".

One word of caution here. When an ad is funny, it has the tendency to have low "connection" to the product it is advertising. That is researcher-speak for people can recall the jokes, but not who brought the ad to them. People remember the talking lizard, but not the insurance company (GEICO) that the commercial was for. So, if you are contemplating a fun/funny communication execution, make sure you check and confirm that your brand recall is as strong as the humor.

Is the Idea Different than the Competition   Fourth, it has to break through the clutter. By this point, we've confirmed that the idea—the product or service you are thinking of developing— is unique. Now, we've got to ensure the communication is perceived that way as well. Honda's "Mr. Opportunity" ads

are an example. They have a cartoon character interacting with humans. Charles Schwab's television commercials start with drawings of people who "morph" into becoming human as the ad goes along.

Does the Message Translate to Sales **Fifth, the communication should lead into interest to buy.** Here, again you can ask consumers how likely they are to purchase your product or service (using the same 11-point purchase scale) based on what they have seen, read or heard in the communication.

Sometimes people ask "isn't this redundant, given that you asked about purchase intent when discussing the potential idea." The answer is no. By this point in the process, you have much more information to give to your target audience. They now know not only what the product is going to look like, but how you are going to communicate its advantages/benefits, where/how you can buy it, at what price point, and so on. The purchase intent score by this point in the process is much more likely to reflect what will happen in the real world, once you launch.

Conclusion

The Innovation Power Score is a way to measure your innovation efforts as you are undertaking them. It will show where there is misalignment between the three circles first mentioned in Chapter 2 and described in Chapters 3, 4, and 5 and it will allow you to take corrective action along the way.

The IPS in Action: An Example

Now that you know how the IPS is constructed, here is a typical scenario to show how you use it, once you have tested the individual components of need, idea, and communication.

Let's go back to the Consumer Packaged Goods (CPG) company that was trying to come up with a product for empowered trailblazers who wanted help in knowing what foods help prevent or counteract what specific health ailments.

After testing countless ideas, they thought they had a winner—an online cookbook that combined recipes with a spreadsheet. Like a typical cookbook, you could look up the recipes you wanted. Say you wanted to make a seven-cheese lasagna. You would type seven-cheese lasagna into the search engine of the CPG's recipe program, and up would pop the recipe. But what was different was you could click on any ingredient called for and find out the "health benefit" for that specific ingredient (e.g., contains soy isoflavones that help ease the symptoms of menopause; contains DHA for brain health; contains eggs that are an excellent source of high-quality protein in addition to choline which some link to improved cognitive functioning, etc.) For example, if you doubled up on the cheese, you would learn what would happen to the overall health function of the dish. Or, you could flip it and call up recipes or foods that were good at addressing specific health benefits (e.g., foods or recipes that are good for reducing cholesterol, for promoting heart health, for helping with sleeplessness, etc.)

Their IPS Score   Remember, if you don't get an IPS score above 80, or one that scores as highly as successful products you have introduced in the past, it is not worth going ahead. In this case, the CPG tested the cookbook-with-spreadsheet idea and came up this Innovation Power Score, a score that is fairly typical:

Insight score: 65 (the bottom of the IPS range)

Idea: 78 (the top of the IPS range)

Communication: 70 (the middle of the IPS range)

Final IPS: 71 (65 + 78 + 70 ÷ 3) = this is the middle of the overall IPS range

The fact that the idea scored highest is not surprising. As we have said from the beginning, coming up with good ideas is relatively easy, so we would expect a solid score here. And the cookbook-with-spreadsheet concept is intriguing. And once you have the idea, communicating what it is (and linking it back to the need) should be a fairly straightforward process.

So would we recommend going ahead and introducing the product into the marketplace? No. For one thing the final IPS score in middle of the IPS database is not great. (Would you be proud of getting a C-, which is about what a 71 in the middle of the database amounts to?) And when we deconstruct that final IPS score, none of the individual components were off the chart. If the Insight had been in the top range and Idea and Communication in the moderate or bottom range, we might conclude the idea was worth pursuing (with possibly an improved/enhanced Idea and definitely a stronger Communication). But the biggest reservation we have is the Insight score is just too low. That tells you that either you have not found the right insight, or that the insight you have discovered is simply not big enough to build a sustainable business around.

> When the insight score is low, it tells you either you have not found the right insight or that the insight you have discovered is simply not big enough to build a sustainable business around.

■ ■ ■

As we said, the results from testing the cookbook-with-spreadsheet idea is a typical case. When you have a disappointing IPS, look to the "need" component, odds are it will be lower than you like. Sometimes, the communication score will be disappointing. That happens fairly often as well, which is easy to explain. Many companies hand off the communication to an outside ad agency or marketing firm, and something about the need or idea gets lost in the process. But most of the time the problem is with the insight. It just isn't strong enough, or reaching a big enough market.

Our recommendation to the client: "Let's go back to the data and see if there are any other compelling needs we could try to execute against."

Three "Frequently Asked Questions" on the Advantages of the IPS

Question #1: "We have more new product ideas around here than I could possibly count. How can the IPS help me know which ones will work?"

Answer: As we mentioned, one of the best things about the IPS is that you can use the big three scores—the insight score, the idea score, and the communication score—either cumulatively or separately. You can look at just the need or idea portions in isolation and that is what we suggest doing here. Is the need big enough? Are there enough people clamoring for the idea you have created to fill the need? If you are not scoring high enough on any one part of the score, our suggestion would be to turn your attention elsewhere.

There is another advantage to using the IPS when you have this kind of problem. By subjecting all the ideas you have to the IPS, you will be able to compare "apples to apples." Even though the concepts you are considering may be wildly different, or developed by various regimes over differing time spans, you will be able to rank them head to head.

Question #2: "I just had a pretty unsuccessful product launch. We thought the product was great. All the research predicted it would do well, but it didn't work out in the real world. I would like to keep my job. Can the IPS help me diagnose what went wrong to keep it from happening again?"

Answer: Yes. It is possible to generate an IPS after the fact. The process is exactly the way it is if you were testing a new product or service idea. The score is constructed by assessing each of the big three scores—need, idea, and communication—separately and then combining them into an overall score. You will be able to see if the need was big enough, whether people wanted your idea (it fulfilled a problem that truly bothered them), and if they understood what you were offering.

We don't want to prejudge anything, but if your research showed you had fulfilled a large need with a compelling idea, the odds are you fell down on the communication.

Question #3: "We have a lot of people involved in the innovation process. And we have a group that comes up with the insights. Then to generate the idea, it goes off to Product Development and R&D, and from there it gets passed on to our communication people to create the marketing material. Not surprisingly, something invariably gets lost in all the translation. How can the IPS help me?"

Answer: The IPS is a tool that management can use to keep all the different people/departments accountable for their role in the new product development process. For those who are responsible for identifying the need, the insight score will ensure you are focusing on the right hole in the marketplace. If you are involved in the idea/service generation, the idea score will show you whether you have invented a blockbuster solution. And for those responsible for making potential customers clearly understand what you have created, the communication score will make sure you have synchronized need and idea. Everyone is accountable for their individual component as well as its contribution to the overall IPS Score.

You Must Remember This

1. **Measure. Measure. Measure.** You need to track each part of the innovation process, not only to make sure you have covered all of your bases but also to guarantee you are creating something new as efficiently as possible.

2. **There are no short cuts.** Some organizations simply ask customers, "do you plan to buy" what we are going to create, and consider their research to be done. If that's all you ask, you are bound to be disappointed when your product or service actually is introduced. You must explore the potential consumers' reaction at every step of the innovation process.

3. **Only high scores are acceptable.** When you test how well you do in the three circles, if you are not scoring in the top quarter, see where you can improve. That's especially true when it comes to the need. If the need isn't big enough, you simply can't make enough money to justify going ahead.

Coming Up Next

The best way to sum up the book is to look in depth at how one company put the principles we have been talking about into practice. The following case study will do just that.

10

Investools: A Case Study in Putting Your Innovation Process to Work

"How does all this work in the real world?"
That's a question we invariably get after we've given a speech explaining how to solve the New Product Paradox.
Our work with Investools is the best answer we have ever come up with.

So far, you have learned about what it takes to innovate successfully and efficiently. As we have shown, overcoming the innovation paradox requires:

- Systematically working your way through the three circles that comprise effective innovation including need, the idea that fulfills the need, and linking the two through communication and commercialization;
- Staying "outside the jar" (i.e., constantly infusing outside thinking into your organization);

- Remaining agnostic about where insights and ideas come from since you can—and should—always subject every idea to extensive testing before you launch;
- Being open to the solution being a product, service, or business model;
- The rigor to do testing and "learn–fail" (learn something from the failure) until you succeed;
- The discipline to follow through, be persistent, and complete the three circles again and again.

It's admittedly not easy, but if you use everything we have talked about, you *will* significantly increase your chances of innovating successfully. (And, at a minimum, gain lots of ground with respect to rounding out your innovation portfolio as we discussed in Chapter 6.)

We have gone through the process piecemeal so, by way of tying it all together, let's see how all the individual components work in harmony using a real example of a company that went through this entire process. (In fact, you will see that they went through it twice.)

Investools' Innovation Paradox

Return with us to those thrilling days of yesteryear [as they used to say during radio shows our grandparents (and great-grandparents) listened to]. Let's go back to the early 2000s. The Internet bubble has burst. Companies like Flooz and Webvan are shutting down and people are returning to the quaint notion that you need a good idea *and* a profitable business model to survive.

And let's suppose you are a very smart CEO of a company that owns what you believe is a very (potentially) lucrative asset—a proprietary tool that lets individual investors and professional traders sort through the tens of thousands of publicly traded stocks, bonds, and currencies out there to uncover opportunities in the marketplace.

Specifically, using a variety of sophisticated trading tools—comprised of both fundamental and technical analysis—this product can take all the data and reduce it to a "buy" or "sell" recommendation. The product works. And back testing shows it would have worked for decades.

That was the good news. The bad news? The CEO, Lee Barba, didn't know what to do with what he had, though he had identified a number of promising ideas including:

- Option 1. A subscription newsletter. The company would hold on to its proprietary software itself, run its findings once a week (for example), and mail the results to subscribers who could decide to act on what the company told them. Because the information was so good, you could charge thousands of dollars per subscription and it would be easy to imagine the newsletter becoming the leader in the category.
- Option 2. Provide the content free to consumers and professional traders, but gain revenue from advertisers based on the demographics of the subscriber base. Just think of all the high-end advertisers—makers of luxury goods, sellers of financial products, upscale hotel chains, the makers of private jets and providers of fractional jet ownership, to name just a few—who would want to reach this customer base.
- Option 3. Education courses. Perhaps there was an opportunity to teach consumers how to use the tool and have them pay for this education on a per-course basis. (One course on how to use the tool to buy stocks; another on how to buy bonds; a third on how to use the tool to purchase options, etc.)
- Option 4. Some kind of combination of the above options.

The options were all intriguing and potentially extremely lucrative. Barba knew he couldn't go after all four. And he also knew he had a company to run day to day and didn't have a lot of time to go down potentially blind alleys. He hired us to help him figure out what would make the most sense.

We explained the three circles to him and agreed that all the ideas he had were intriguing, but that wasn't the place to start. We need to find out whether he had discovered a need that customers would want filled. So our first priority/job was to go back to the first circle—need—and answer some core questions.

- How should we define success?
- What are the consumer segments/targets of opportunity?
- What problems/tensions do they have (i.e., what insights could we identify)?
- And what opportunities do those present?

Only then could we help him pick a business model that made sense.

And so we went to work. Figuring out how the company would define success was straightforward: As far as the CEO was concerned, this was all about the stock price. If the company did well, and earnings increased, that would boost the share price and be the CEO's' primary determinant of success. As for what the market wanted, we needed to find out.

Circle #1

So we did what the first circle told us to do: We spent a lot of time discovering what was out there. Not surprisingly, we found a lot of companies offering product and services similar to what Investools could, but none had Investools' method of analyzing the stock, bond, and currencies markets.

More important, among the target audience, we found out there was a huge need. There were literally millions of novice and relatively new investors who said they wanted simple, objective advice they could use on their way to becoming much more educated about the best ways to handle their money. And experienced traders were looking for ways to double check the advice they were getting from their brokers and other financial advisors.

Out of this research came an early hypothesis: People spend tens of thousands of dollars educating themselves, earning GEDs, college degrees, and post-graduate degrees. Thousands of hours of effort go into preparing ourselves for better jobs through training, supplemental education courses, and the like. Yet, very little of the education resources—time and money—we invest is devoted to how to save/invest our money.

The irony is overwhelming. Many people graduate from the top-tier MBA programs and still don't know the difference between a Roth or traditional IRA, how best to allocate their portfolio between stocks and bonds, international versus domestic investments, or whether to buy Google or Apple stock based on their risk/reward profile.

The insight was strikingly clear and we put it into the format we have used throughout this book:

> I want to **secure my financial future** because I want to **live fully,** but today there is **no single trustworthy place** that I can go to for help becoming a better investor.

We had found the need. We then followed this research with a large, in-depth quantitative survey to understand how many people had that need and found the answer was "a lot." Our hypothesis was confirmed.

When we dug a little deeper we found there were two sizable segments we could go after. On one end of the spectrum were "eager learners," people who wanted to know as much as possible about managing their money. They were already spending on financial education, and they were willing to spend a lot more. Although they accounted for just 20 percent of the market, they represented 39 percent of the potential value because they were such heavy users of educational materials.

And on the other end of the spectrum, were the "sage investors," people who were already quite savvy about the financial markets, but wanted more tools to become even more successful and possibly become full-time traders.

Back then these people represented just less than a fifth of the market, but more than a third of the potential profits.

These findings confirmed again there was a need. The need and insight is real, sizable, and currently unmet. (Of course there were competitors in this space but no one occupied the upper tiers of education. Instead "get-rich-quick" was more the norm.) It was time to figure how we could go about filling it. It was time to move on to the second circle.

Circle #2

Now that we had the target (eager learners and sage investors) and the insight, it was time to think through the variety of new products, services, and business models.

We began to ideate/brainstorm, complete with lots of outside experts from the entertainment industry (who knows better how to reach a vast audience?), university professors (who knows more about teaching?), as well as Internet leaders (a possible delivery vehicle). Just about all the ideas we kept coming up with to alleviate the tension we had found in the insight kept leading us to the same place: We needed to create some kind of financial planning university.

When we tested the idea we found not only did consumers love it, they refined it. For one thing, they didn't want a run-of-the-mill financial college, they wanted the "Harvard of Investment Education."

But how would it work in practice? What courses would we offer; in what forum (typical class instruction, online, a combination); in what forum (one course at a time; should it be like going to college, where you take a handful of courses a semester) and of course, at what price? In other words, what exactly should the idea look like?

We went to potential customers and asked them about all these options, and there was a clear, overwhelming preference. They wanted the offerings to be exactly like a college. There could be beginning education (B.A.) to expert (Ph.D.). That was the big finding from talking to potential customers. They didn't want to take individual courses. They wanted the level of content they needed (beginner, immediate, advanced—that is, B.A., Master, Ph.D.) to be all bundled together. And they told us that they were willing to pay a lot for it: $3,000 for the basic—"B.A."-level education—up to $25,000 for the advanced one—the Ph.D.

We now had a huge need and a compelling idea to fill it and Barba had the managerial expertise to create a company that could build what customers wanted. Now, we had to communicate to people what we were going to offer them.

Circle #3

While almost nothing about innovation is linear and obvious, the communication component in this case was straightforward That should not have been surprising. Why? Because we had done all the homework. We knew the target. We knew the competitive differentiation (how we could make our offering unique compared to everything out there). Now it was "just" a matter of creating the communication.

We knew the product, all the features including price, positioning, benefits, and reasons to believe. We now had to communicate this externally to our core consumers via the web, direct mail, and direct response TV.

After walking through all the steps of the third circle, which we discussed in detail in Chapter 5, the message we went with was: Here's how to secure your financial future. Our potential audience had told us: a) they knew that they were ultimately responsible for their finances, and b) they were willing to do the hard work required to be financially secure, if someone would just provide them with the tools.

We created high-end marketing materials that could easily have come from an Ivy League institution. We sent CDs with terrific production values and every communication we did sent the subliminal message, "this is a top-of-the-line organization."

It worked. The communication clearly linked the need with the idea and resonated with customers. Literally thousands of people signed up for the courses—with a significant number going through all three levels of education. The payoff from all this? The stock, which was trading at 23 cents a share, rose to $3.40 within 18 months.

If You Did It Once . . .

A couple of years later, the phone rings and it was Lee Barba once again and, smart guy that he is, he has another idea, and asks us to help him reinvent his company for a second time.

Because of the earlier work of creating the "Harvard of Investment Education" the company had "graduated" thousands of investors who had gone on to become very successful traders once they had finished the company's courses. But, the problem from Investools' perspective was that they were not benefiting from their graduates' success. While it did get a referral fee for sending its graduates to brokerage firms if they wanted to trade based on what they had learned from their courses, that fee was: a) small, and b) a one-time thing.

The idea Barba wanted us to help him with? Creating Investools' own trading solution. He wanted us to tell him if it was feasible for Investools to educate customers and then help those students execute the trades they wanted to make, once they had the requisite knowledge.

But wait! Is that crossing the line? Did Investools' graduates believe in the separation of church and state (which in this case means "you can't teach me to trade on the one hand and then on the other make money on the trades you taught me to make. There appears to be an inherent bias.")

Well, it was possible that Investools graduates didn't believe there was a bias and could see the value in "one-stop shopping." But even if they did there were a myriad of SEC regulations that the company would have to comply with before it would be allowed to execute trades.

In short, there were a lot of questions that had to be answered by the CEO's intriguing question. But, once again we knew where we were: in the second circle! We had a potentially commercial idea, but we needed to go back to the first circle and ask ourselves: What are we solving for? What insight are we delivering a solution for? What will our customers believe/say? What is it that they want/need?

When it comes to the process, you know what happens next. We went back to the first circle and did our research: competitive landscape analysis, in-depth consumer work, and the like. And not only did a strong majority of Investools' customers—and people who were likely to become Investools customers—not object to the company adding a trading component, they wanted it. They told us that they liked the simplicity—if they found a stock or bond they thought was a bargain, after using the Investools' analysis, they wanted to be able to buy it immediately. And they also liked the idea of one company handling everything, not only the education component but executing the investment strategy as well.

So, we had found a need. Now it was a matter of testing the idea, which of course took us to the second circle. What should the trading platform do? What elements should be— and legally (SEC) could be—integrated? How much should we charge? What is the best way to fold it into Investools' existing operations?

Now it was time to execute this solution and deliver it to students. Both parts are extremely important. The best innovation concept in the world will still fail, if you fail to execute well. And, as we have talked about throughout, if people don't understand what you have, they probably aren't going to buy it.

When it came to execution, the biggest decision was should Investools build a trading capability from scratch, or partner with someone else? That turned out to be a fairly easy decision. Many companies already offered this functionality and starting from scratch made little sense. Thinkorswim was one of the most efficient brokers and provided the ideal trading platform for the students that wanted it. The integration went smoothly.

As for the communication effort, after extensive testing with consumers, the company went with the straightforward message "integrating the best trading tools possible." And the outcome this time? The stock more than tripled in two years and the company was eventually sold to TD Ameritrade for half a billion dollars.

Conclusion

So what is the lesson? Is innovation really as easy as the Investools story makes it seem? No, for a couple of reasons. One, what we described here in a couple of thousand words took place over nearly a decade. Second, this is a case where things worked out just like everyone hoped.

As we have seen throughout this book, that doesn't usually happen. Many times new concepts are killed before they are introduced into the marketplace because subjecting them to The Innovation Power Score shows they are simply not going to be successful.

But what the Investools story does do is show us that having a fully integrated innovation process works if you are disciplined about moving your way through the three circles. You need to be mindful of taking a "portfolio" approach to innovation—balancing evolutionary and revolutionary innovation opportunities—and be willing to let the market tell you if you are right.

■ ■ ■

At this point, we want to wish you good luck as you put what you have learned into practice. But, if you follow the three circles as you go about constructing your innovation process, you will need that luck far less than most.

Acknowledgments

We coach our clients and friends that intelligence is learning from one's own mistakes but wisdom is learning from the mistakes of others. So we ask them to create "learning cultures," not "knowing cultures" (as in "we know everything; there is nothing more we can learn.") We ask them to be wise not smart.

We were wise when we put together this book.

That brings us to our next bit of coaching: parallel engineer anything you possibly can. (Parallel engineering sounds much more consultative than "stealing" and we fashion ourselves quite consultative.)

Nearly 20 years of parallel engineering went into this book. While it is impossible to thank all of the clients individually for the trust they put in the hands of Maddock Douglas, please know that we are incredibly grateful. Thank you.

Thanks, also, to the many inventive people at Maddock Douglas. You've all helped create a platform that inspires and empowers curious people—and in large part made this book possible.

Thanks to Paul B. Brown who asked so many great questions and was so generous with his wonderful ability to create simple lessons from complex experiences.

Thanks to Ainslie Simmonds whose leadership on both sides of the desk has helped us to be as wise as we are fearless.

Thanks to McRae Williams for always being ready with a "truth bomb" when one was necessary.

Thanks to Raphael Louis Viton (that's his stage name) for providing the operational balance that kept the "idea monkeys" from running the innovation circus.

Thanks to Lee Barba. We referenced his company's success but it would not have happened if he wasn't so courageous when it came to new ideas.

Finally, a special thanks to our spouses for their patience, love, and understanding.

Index